Optimize Wellness and Maximize Life

OPTIMIZE IS THE HEALTH SIDE & MAXIMIZE IS THE GROWTH SIDE

MARY AXNESS, N.D.

NOTE TO READER

This book contains information that is not designed to take the place of, substitute, or replace any form and method of professional or medical advice and treatment or medicine. All content is the author's opinion and is not intended to diagnose or to treat diseases. The facts and figures contained in this document are presented solely for informational and educational purposes only.

This book contains materials compiled from various resources and sources considered accurate and deemed reliable to the best of the author's knowledge; however, the author cannot guarantee its validity or held accountable for any omissions or errors. The contents of this book are periodically updated.

This disclaimer covers any injury or damages resulting from the application and uses, whether indirectly or directly, from any information or advice that are given, whether criminal intent, personal injury, negligence, offence, contract breach, or any action caused. To ensure your safety and health, consult a medical or professional practitioner before applying any of the information, techniques, advice, and remedies mentioned in this document.

DEDICATION

---◆---

To The Holy Spirit,
my Greatest Counselor, Teacher, & Comforter
I would like to dedicate this first book to all who imprinted my
heart to become: My Father's Daughter, with Christ Jesus:

Dr. John & Ornetta Bergstrom, nearly 50 years you reintroduced
me to the best image of what an earthly father should be.
Dr. Gerald Ellison, still percolating my heart to journal, write and
publish, countless hours of reframing when you called out the hidden
gold in me. Pastor Margaret Hawthorne who showed me a life of prayer
and prophesied that I would be in nutrition, and will be connected to
just the right one, Dr. Joel Robbins, the real Doctor who showed up
and challenged me, you were the mistral helped making
Part I - A dream realized.
Pastor Billy Joe Daughtery, your commanding presence provoked me to
attend Victory Bible College. Mrs. Iru Daughtery, you pursued me with
your "Won't Let Go" hugs. Pastor Sharon Daughtery who exemplifies
bold faith daily to her flock: you anchor the stars, Thank you, Ron
McIntosh, Dr. Edwin Miranda, jr., at Victory Bible College.

Dr. Leif Hetland, your teachings usher the father's nurturing heart,
inspiring me to keep identity. BASSM, Steve and Lindy Hale, Jenn
Stockman-my voice matters and Blake Healy,
your persevering faith unlocked my file cabinets.
Countless unstoppable women and orphans, who served along me
ferociously courageous in the dungeons and in/out of prisons.

Mom and dad, I see your thumbs up, we shall meet again!
My 45 years-one and only, Mark, you're supporting and supplying,
your vigilant editing, you have kept me from stir-frying my laptop.
To my children, Katie and Andy, Nate and Christian,
so glad you allow me to gather His stars,
Andersen and Ella, you are the dreams and the twinkling stars,
my reasons to publish my legacy writings.

Despina and Rowen, thankful for your creative supports
Finally, my special friend and sister Jonnie Sue Williams, your
relentlessness to correct my rambling on. Patiently helped the
completion of this writing possible, So grateful for your supports.

ENDORSEMENTS

---◆---

I have known Mary since 1972, she has achieved an amazing life and career. She has a solid marriage and two wonderful children. She is a nutritionist focusing on exemplifying a legacy and epitomizing a Woman of Wisdom. You will be amazed with the depth and thoroughness of her understanding of wholeness; both physically and mentally, she has walked the walk, now you will glean from her understanding of health and living. As a believer, husband, father, dental and prosthodontic specialist born in 1935. I have had a lifetime of experience in all areas of life. Mary is a naturopathic doctor and an ordained minister. She helps to bring clarity, awareness of who you are and whose you belong to. I give my unconditional endorsement of this book. You will be pleased!

John Bergstrom B.S., M.S., D.D.S., Prosthodontics

North Dakota State University, University of Minnesota

Dr. Axness highlights the importance of learning from life's experiences, especially in the context of health and faith. From these paths of intrigue, Dr. Mary inspires both aspects as she captures rare and honest cultural insights, practical wisdom and the pursuit of wholeness. She generously shares with her readers personal growth, maximizing life and her healing miracles. Once we invest into this new insight, we will appreciate the mind of one of God's chosen.

Bishop James R. Jackson, Ph.D., Pastoral Counselor,
Founder/Chancellor LYFE Theological Seminary

I have known Dr. Mary for over 7 years as a mentor and friend. She has always encouraged and challenged me to pursue excellence in my career, as a leader and in my personal life. I have had transformative experiences at her events. I am forever grateful for Mary's friendship and wisdom. You will enjoy the authenticity of her teaching and stories.

Sandy Deer, Director, Human Resources, Certified Life Coach

FOREWORD

It is with great pleasure and admiration that I write this foreword for this professional nutritionist, Mary Axness, N.D., whose words you are about to embark upon. In a world where diet trends come and go, and nutritional information seems to change in the blink of an eye, having a trusted expert to guide us is invaluable.

Nutrition plays a pivotal role in our overall well-being, affecting not only our physical health but also our mental and emotional states. In this fast-paced era, where convenience often takes precedence over nourishment, it is refreshing to encounter a professional nutritionist who is dedicated to empowering individuals with the knowledge, and tools necessary to make informed choices about lifestyle wellness.

Throughout the pages of this book, you will find a wealth of evidence-based information, practical advice, and insightful guidance in every story. Dr. Mary's deep understanding of the complex interplay between food and our bodies shines through, as she elucidates the importance of balanced nutrition, and personalized approaches to health. She does not expect an immediate and drastic change, rather she suggests just a one-degree change can have an impactful and profound improvement in your overall health and healing.

What sets Dr Mary, as we lovingly call her, apart as a nutritionist is her unwavering commitment to science-backed recommendations. In an age where pseudoscience and fad diets often dominate the conversation, it is refreshing to witness an expert who champions evidence-based practices and encourages critical thinking when it comes to nutrition.

Moreover, her compassionate and empathetic approach is evident in every chapter. She understands that nutrition is not a one-size-fits-all endeavor and that everyone's journey toward optimal health is unique. By encouraging self-compassion and emphasizing the importance of sustainable lifestyle changes, she inspires readers to embark on a lifelong path of wellness from the inside out, rather than chasing short-term fixes.

My personal experience with Dr. Mary is as a semi-retired Educator of almost seventy-four years old, who in the last six years have taken on acquiring an additional Doctorate, running an Education Consultant practice, teaching online education courses, working with foster and adoptive families to improve Social Service interactions, in addition to adopting two sibling girls oldest now 14 years old and her sister now 6 years old that I have had since birth requires mental stability, energy, and fortitude. Dr. Mary's wise and simple adjustments to my normal food routines help to provide the extra fuel and potentially increased longevity, I need to maintain my mental capacity, energy, and busy lifestyle, while also correcting internally some of the unknown nutritional abuses I have inflicted on my own body.

This book is not just a compendium of nutritional knowledge; it is a roadmap to transforming one's relationship with food and lifestyle of wholistic awareness to untangle the cause of the body's deficiencies, adding to the possibility of maintaining lasting health. She brings into focus principles with mandates as living proof that science is catching up in understanding lifestyle wellness by design. You will expand your capacity through the accompanying practical stories in this book. Whether you are a seasoned health enthusiast or a novice seeking to make positive changes, the wisdom contained within these pages will undoubtedly enlighten and empower you.

I am honored to have the opportunity to introduce you to this remarkable professional and her invaluable insights. Prepare to be inspired, educated, and motivated to take charge of your health and your relationships in a way that aligns with your unique needs and aspirations.

With her guidance, may you embark on a transformative journey toward a nourished and vibrant life.

Sincerely,
Dr. Yvette P. W. Mitchell, CEO
ESI- Education Services and Learning Institute

TABLE OF CONTENTS

———————◆———————

PART I

OPTIMIZE WELLNESS

CHAPTER 1

INTRODUCTION
COMPLIMENTARY AND
FUNCTIONAL

———◆———

Complimentary and Preventative: Naturopathy or naturo-pathic medicine was the earlies known healing system. Before surgery and synthetic isolation of chemical substances, foods, water, and whole herbs were used by many cultures for wide range of health issues. For example, The Chinese used kelp over 3,000 years ago for thyroid health, now in the West, its called TCM, Traditional Chinese Medicine. Ancient Egyptians used liver for night blindness. Native American culture uses various herbs to promote and maintain healing.

Traditional medicine or Western Medicine: Primarily is to handle life-threatening disease and/or crises. Traditional medicine does not help with the prevention of disease.

Natural medicine, Functional medicine or Complementary medicine which include Naturopathy. The goal is not to do away with traditional medicine, but rather bring needed support that is complementary with following purpose in mind:

- Preventive in nature (before symptom show up).
- Attempt to restore health from the state of dis-ease.
- Do all we can to reverse, to slow or halt an actual disease process
- Attend to nutritional deficiencies
- Deal with toxicity which cause nutrition and physical degeneration: Detox

In 2006 I began seeing a naturopathic doctor when my personal crisis finally subsided, and I had regained back the healthy weight. Dr. Joel Robbins showed up at my office, introduced himself and gifted me one of his CD teaching, the rest is history. I followed up with an appointment, and he asked what were my symptoms and because I had none, he questioned why I wanted the appointment. My reply was that I only have one body with many parts, a complex and an amazing machine, I do not take my health for granted or leave it to chance, especially after a life or death episode in July, 1999. I also prefer not to wait for a disease to shows up! Plus, I want to go toward the next level of health. Subsequently, I graduated from the College of Natural Health, initially as a nutrition coach, then continue and I completed the naturopathic degree as an N.D., I then attended multiple Chef educational schools and seminars, handling food as nutrition, serving at the Tulsa Integrative Clinic headed by Dr. B. (Deceased), Dr. Joel Robbins, other clinicians and therapists. plus a few auxiliary specialties. Previously trained in skincare in the U.S. and Japan. I served mostly by referrals from cosmetic related dental and plastic surgeons.

I was so blessed to have worked with excellent professionals, started with my favorite dentist, since 1972 my American Dad, Dr. John C. Bergstrom, his gentleness helped removed the childhood fear of dentistry. Through being around many of them, I got a chance to observe and ask questions. I had been reading many health books, nutrition books, from weight loss to weight gain. Cooking and creating herbal culinary cuisines, they are very therapeutic, adding to my well being. Also many unending subjects on Spirituality, emotional health, and inner healing trainings and practices around the country as a recipient and a minister.

What came to my mind was that we are not dissected beings, westerners tend to compartmentalize their lives as fractioned beings I strongly believe compartmentalizing our being results in so much confusion. We are human beings living out the birthright to be a unified whole person in whom these parts are not separate entities, but interconnected and unified, physically, mentally and emotionally and spiritually. Health is our blessed design, and we are the temple of God.

Subsconciously, we put on many hats with many undertakings on various functions. We are sons and daughters, moms and dads, siblings, parents, uncles, aunties, grandparents, neighbors and so on. Our works call us into many levels of relationships because we are surrounded by interesting people. Eating at many gatherings and are typically customary so there is no getting around it. Many of us 50 and over are in the "Sandwich generation." As caregivers, continuing every task, as we put most everything inside our bodies, but how do our delivery system transport and get the nutrients each body requires.

A true state of health and wellness may only be accomplished through intentionally supporting the body's own healing mechanisms as well as by renewing our minds to live life to the highest potentials. Like it or not, we now are in a time of taking personal responsibility in terms of prioritizing our internal landscapes: We must make many choices to advance our goals of caring for ourselves and loved ones all around. The body and the soul are dynamically knitted together. One part does intricately affect other parts of our total makeup. We will do well to treat the body, mind and emotions more as a whole unit. Thus, when looking at the word wholesome, it behooves us to see the "whole" as a "some" of the totality of a magnificent design passionately from love. God forbid that we live lives as segmented or compartmentalized beings. You may need clarity in today's wide spectrum of wellness world. Until then, let us give this amazing self-healing body the best chance to thrive not just survive. As you walk through the pages, imagine with me the aromatic fragrance of the fresh herbs, we ought to consume fuel for the body's best performance, while occasionally enjoy rich foods.

Part I is what you can do to pick your one degree of change, try something new every week. If you already know it all, select a theme to enhance your wellness. Part II is about living a healed and whole prospective, from identity and from love. Forgiven to forgive, be free and be an asset to those who matters around you.

CHAPTER 2
ACTIVITIES & EDIBLE WELLNESS

———————◆———————

Superfoods: You heard it! Anyone can tell you, eat your greens, let me explain why we need them and know there are more to choose from. Since Covid pandemic, mid 2020, it appears that a flood gate has opened for explosive information regarding herbs and superfoods, and people's increasing appetites for personal health and wellness has increased exponentially. As a child, my parents prepared foods only for health reasons. I asked what are mushrooms good for? All I heard was that it cleans up unwanted garbage inside. Today, we know it's an antioxidant and an effective detoxifier, mushroom draw upon whatever is decaying in the blood or in the respiratory system. Many Americans are attempting to use superfoods since the pandemic. The interests with herbal medicine are absolutely needed for immunotherapy purposes. I must caution you, the reader, Herbal medicine are very potent, please consult a professional for dosing and contradictions until you acquire some basic knowledge of why you want to incorporate this superfood into your diet. Also, beware of contraindication when interacting with personal prescription medications.

Mushroom Therapies:

There are many different types of edible mushrooms, each with its own unique taste and nutritional profile. In my medicinal herbal textbooks: Interaction of mushroom rich in beta-glucans with certain receptor may even be able to "train" to improve the body's own innate immune response. Bone, Kerry *Functional Herbal Therapy, A modern Paradigm for Clinicians.* Aeon Books, 2021 London.

Some of the more popular edible mushrooms generally most Americans will find delightful adding to their diets, they include:

1. Button Mushrooms. These are the most common types of mushrooms found in your local grocery stores. They are low in calories and fat, and are a good source of protein, fiber and B vitamins.

2. Shiitake Mushrooms: These mushrooms have a rich, smoky flavor and are a good source of protein, fiber, and several vitamins and rich in minerals, including copper, manganese, and zinc. Also known to stimulate your immune system. A form of beta-glucans in Shiitake mushroom, it is a favorite for vegetarian ideally uses them as meat substitute, very flavorful when added to seafood, poultry and meat dishes.

3. Portobello mushrooms: These are large, meaty mushrooms that are often used as a vegetarian substitute for meat. They are an excellent source of protein, fiber and several vitamins and minerals, including selenium and potassium.

4. Oyster Mushrooms: There mushrooms have a delicate, nutty flavor and are a good source of protein, fiber, and several vitamins and minerals, including iron, zinc, and potassium too.

5. Reishi Mushroom: Traditional Chinese Medicine regards Reishi as an energy, tonifying agent for the body and increasing memory. Supportive to liver and it helps to increase metabolic rate of enzyme activity. Mostly use for steeping for tea or cook as broth. It's not so much for eating but for medicinal use.

6. Lion's Mane, a shaggy looking fungi food for the brain and boost cognitive functions. It has a seafood flavor, but rather expensive and is revered for its regenerative for stimulating nerve growth factor.

And there are so many more versions of edible mushrooms, including psychedelic mushrooms now becoming legalized in the Northwest coastal regions of United States. In addition to their unique taste, edible mushrooms offer many other health benefits. They are a good source of antioxidants, which can help to protect the body from damage caused by free radicals. They are also a great source of beta-glucans, a soluble fiber that has been shown to boost immune function and lower cholesterol levels.

Some studies have also suggested that consuming mushrooms may have anti-cancer properties and could help reduce the risk of development of certain types of cancers.

It is most import to note that while many types of mushrooms are safe to eat, some are extremely poisonous and can cause death if consumed cooked or raw. Be sure you purchase edible mushrooms from your local grocers or from a reputable source, there are mushroom experts that teach how to identify various species of mushrooms. (GreenMed info Research Group)

How to clean mushrooms:

A word about preparing for mushrooms, you cannot clean them well enough. The best and safe way is to soak them in at 1 quart of water mixed with 1-2 tablespoons of white vinegar (let it sit and soak for 30 minutes or a couple of hours before consumption, raw or cooked).

Mushrooms have a long history of use in Asian cultures, where they have been highly valued for their medicinal properties and nutritional benefits for a few thousands of years. Many traditional Chinese and Japanese medicines include various species dated back to the Han Dynasty (206 BCE-200 CE), where they were used to promote longevity and improve stamina as well as overall health. Mushrooms such as Rishi (Ganoderma Lucidum) and shiitake (Lentinula edodes) were highly valued for reduction of inflammation, and their ability to boost immunity. I use mushrooms as a regular dietary basic, not everyone likes the aroma of the dishes unless you are Asian, they can be pricy.

In Japan, mushrooms have been a dietary staple also for centuries. Japanese have a long tradition of cultivating mushrooms, and they have developed a unique culinary culture around them. Mushrooms are commonly used in Japanese cooking and are some of the healthiest foods in the world.

Agaricus Mushrooms:

Agaricus mushrooms are classified as a powerful superfood, their constituents and health benefits are mainly consumed for their medicinal properties and nutritional benefits for centuries. There are many species of Agaricus mushrooms, but the most well-known and extensively studied is Agaricus Blazei, also known as Agaricus subrufescens or the "mushroom of the sun".

It is worth noting that while Agaricus mushrooms are generally considered safe and non-toxic, they may cause allergic reactions in some individuals, it can be contradicted for people who are on blood-thinning medications, a little will go a long way especially in powder form. Again, please consult a medical professional before you consider using any mushroom therapies. Finally, I incorporate mushroom as a diet therapy in a powder form with tissue healing especially for adults. Agaricus is not the type of mushroom you find in kitchens because of its high cost. The safest type of mushrooms is mentioned in the bullet sections, four type especially for new taste buds.

Psychedelic Mushrooms: Now this therapy involves highly skilled herbalist with a medical degree and be sure to check that your insurance provider will cover the consultation for this therapeutic treatment.

This is appearing like the latest and greatest medicinal herb, Rivaling Tribulus (works well for women and men.) Tongkat Ali (Eurycoma Longifolia) is a well-known traditional plant in Southeast Asia where it has been used for centuries, the roots are popular among Malaysians traditionally use it to maintain sexual interest. Many men imagined themselves aging healthy. Maintaining muscle mass, fitness, vitality. Men who suffer with poor energy, sedentary lifestyles, and loss of libido, supporting vitality and stamina. General sense of well-being. Contraindications are not well known. May increase levels of testosterone, could potentially worsen hormone-sensitive cancers. Consult your physicians if you have prostate, ovarian or breast cancer, if you have a history of liver disease due to hepatotoxic effects. May also interact with certain medications including blood thinners:

- Reducing stress, anxiety and improving mood.

- Boosting athletic performance and may increase muscle mass.

- Support fat loss by reducing appetite.

Some simple herbs to consider that you may hear of Ginger throughout part I, for Asian culture, ginger is not optional. It is of the highest culinary and medicinal value. I use ginger every day, and I demonstrate how to prepare anti-inflammation dishes as well as drinks for my personal go to edible wellness regimes.

Aloe Vera is antiseptic, antimicrobial, and anti-inflammatory as well as rich in amino acids and minerals, such as in calcium, copper, iron, phosphorus, potassium, and zinc. Raw aloe vera gel is a phytonutrient superfood, it contains live enzymes as well as essential fatty acids that are excellent in alleviating headaches induced by acidic foods. Aloe's polysaccharide action on fibroblast multiplies adding to their hydrating properties for skin rejuvenation. (Mix raw honey and with fresh Aloe Vera gel, I drink this as often as several times a week whenever I can.) Father Romano Zago, a Franciscan Priest authored a book "Cancer can be cured!" (USA) quantumnutrition.com, (Italy) aloedipadreromanozago.it

Essiac formula, taken in tea form, a known immune-enhancing herbal formulation comprised of several well-known herbs, namely Burdock Root, Slippery Elm Barks, Sheep Sorrel Leaves and Indian Rubard Root. The combined effects are for GI Immunity, mucus elimination, as well as kidney and liver detox. Essiac herbal formula that has been in use since the formula was given to nurse Renee Casey Caisse from a Canadian Objiawaj Indian, in 1922. Her original herbal formula preparation into a drink called Essiac Herbal Supplement was given to thousands at her clinic in Brace bridge, Ontario, Canada. **Nurse Rene Caisse continues to be loved and remembered for her contribution to naturopathic medicine at the Canadian College of Naturopathic Medicine in Toronto. mailto:essiac@essiacproducts.com

<u>Ginger</u> is high in anti-inflammatory properties for osteo-arthritis especially joint pains, and sore muscles post workouts. For centuries, ginger has been used to treat symptoms of colds and flu. Ginger is high in antioxidants and can boost metabolism. Drinking warm water with drops of fresh squeezed ginger juice can help eliminate nausea and support the immune system, it is the best remedy for post-surgery recovery. Steeping a few slices of fresh ginger root in your morning lemon water routine can promote circulation.

Cautions for ginger users, please keep a close monitor of your bowel movements if you are new to using ginger. Do <u>be cautious if you have bile production or gallstone issues</u>.

<u>Lemon Balm</u>, good to use as tea, has mild meditative effect and ease of anxiety. Caution, not to take high dose for prolonged intake of this herb can have opposite effects.

<u>Turmeric</u> is part of the ginger family, in Indian cuisines, curcumin is a powerful antioxidant. Supports both blood and circulation and tones the liver and spleen. It has one of the highest anti-inflammatory properties,

its yellow pigment provides the richest sources of beta-carotene, almost none of the concerns of contraindications compared with other herbs. More and more research has shown promising regarding help for diabetes. However, turmeric is not for large quantities consumption at one given time.

Green Tea is rich in Theanine, and is structurally like glutathione, also having a very high antioxidant effect. It can be highly stimulating and depending on the health of your adrenal glands, therefore important not to overdose resulting in overstress the systemic homeostasis.

Hydrogen Peroxide - 35% Food Grade can do many wonders.

Adding 5-seven drops of food grade hydrogen peroxide to one gallon of distilled or reverse osmosis water, this can turn your drinking water to taste like fresh spring water. Use caution when handling hydrogen peroxide, use gloves or it can burn the skin.

*Do not use hydrogen peroxide if you have well water that's high in iron or copper.

Fermented Foods, for quality digestive health. We need quality of gut flora, the good bacteria, foods produced or preserved by actions of microorganisms. Fermentation process turns sugar to alcohol using yeast. Other fermenting processes involve using bacteria such as lactobacillus in yogurt and sauerkraut. Some pickled or soured foods are also fermented foods, some processed with brine, vinegar, garlic, or acid such as lemon juice.

In the US, we generally purchase "Probiotics" which are marketed as food supplements. Lactobacillus acidophilus is one of the most common types of probiotics and can be found in fermented foods, yogurt (most have added sugar), and supplements section at your market.

What is Lactobacillus Acidophilus? Lactobacillus acidophilus is a type of bacteria found in your intestines. It's a member of the Lactobacillus genus of bacteria, and it plays an important role in human health. Its name gives an indication of what it produces — lactic acid. It does this by producing an enzyme called lactase. Lactase breaks down lactose, a sugar found in milk, into lactic acid. Lactobacillus acidophilus is also sometimes referred to as L. acidophilus or simply acidophilus. There are in addition to probiotic supplements, L. acidophilus can be found naturally in several fermented foods, including sauerkraut, miso, and tempeh. Also, it's added to other foods like certain cheese and a similar study found that L. acidophilus alone also may reduce abdominal pain. On the other hand, a study that examined a mixture of L. acidophilus and other probiotics found that it had no effect in helping IBS symptoms. This might be explained by another study suggesting that taking a low dose of single-strain probiotics for a short duration may improve IBS symptoms the most. Probiotics may be effective for weight loss, but more research is needed to determine whether L. acidophilus has a significant effect on weight in humans. Healthy bacteria like L. acidophilus can boost the immune system and thus help reduce the risk of viral infections. In fact, some studies have suggested that probiotics may prevent and improve symptoms of the common cold.

Another study carefully examined the effects of L. acidophilus on the gut. It found that taking it as a probiotic increased the expression of genes (this is very generalized statement.) in the intestines that are involved in the immune response. These results suggest that L. acidophilus may support a healthy immune system. A separate study examined how the combination of L. acidophilus and a prebiotic affected human gut health. It was found that the combined supplement increased the amounts of lactobacilli and Bifidobacterium in the intestines, as well as branched-chain fatty acids, which are an important part of a healthy gut. A well-regulated gut microbiome goes a long way to prevent disease.

Probiotics, prebiotics, and a combination that is <u>symbiotic</u>, have been reported to modulate gut microbiota of humans. However, it's also found in a number of foods, particularly <u>fermented foods</u>. Most foreign countries, most traditions enjoy home-made fermented foods rather than purchasing probiotic supplements from the store. The best food sources of L. acidophilus are the human microbiome conditions largely influences by your long-term dietary pattern consistent by the nutrients.

Below are all helpful probiotic foods to consider:

1. **Yogurt**: Yogurt is typically made from bacteria such as *L. bulgaricus* and *S. thermophilus*. Some yogurts also contain *L. acidophilus*, but only those that list it in the ingredients and state "live and active cultures."

2. **Kefir**: Kefir is made of "grains" of bacteria and yeast, which can be added to milk or water to produce a healthy fermented drink.

The types of bacteria and yeast in kefir can vary, but it commonly contains *L. acidophilus*, among others.

3. **Miso:** Miso is a paste originating from Japan that is made by fermenting soybeans. Although the primary microbe in miso is a fungus called *Aspergillus oryzae*, miso can also contain many bacteria, including *L. acidophilus*.

4. **Tempeh:** Tempeh is another food made from fermented soybeans. It can contain several different microorganisms. A traditional soy product originally from Indonesia made by natural culturing that binds soybeans into a cake form. including *L. acidophilus*.

5. **Beer:** A traditional alcoholic beverage (depending on recipes) is made from grains and hops.

6. **Chinese Rice Sugar Sponge Cake:** Many Asian Children treat it as a dessert, it tastes sweet but with a tangy sour flavor to it. As a child I had no idea the rice sugary spongy cake for gut health.

7. **Yakult:** A brand of sour milk, which is packaged like a convenient food, good for the skin.

8. **Kimchi:** Popular in Korea is gaining much popularity in the US. Mainly consist of Chinese Napa Cabbage, garlic, chili paste, and sea salt.

9. **Fermented Bean Paste:** Famous in cuisines of Southeast Asia, a type of miso, but used in stir fried foods.

10. **Kombucha:** Fermented tea, needs a "Mother/or Scoby," Sugar and Black Tea, very refreshing when adding apples, or various fruits or lemon slices.

11. **Cheese**: Different varieties of cheese are produced by using different bacteria. *L. acidophilus* is not commonly used as a cheese starter culture, but several studies have examined the effects of adding it as a probiotic.

12. **Salgam**: From Turkey, it is a very popular beverage from southern Turkey. Made with juice of carrot, pickles, salt, spiced and flavored with turnips. Fermented and aged in barrels which is very aromatic in flavor.

13. **Shark Meat**: Shark meat can be fermented along, just like fish sauce, made from fermented anchovy, I use fish source instead of soy sauce more these days.

14. **Natto**: Famous in Japan, Natto is a traditional Japanese food made from soybeans. Fermented with Bacillus subtills var. Natto. Often served as a breakfast food. Mixing with mustard and soy sauce and bunching onion. Natto may be an acquired taste due to its strong flavor. After a couple of tries, I began to crave natto with my fresh cooked rice. Natto has the bioavailable form of Vitamin K2 when combined with D3, it's very helpful for building bone density, especially for arthritic joints, overwhelming promising studies are more available now.

15. **Sour Cream**: Obtained by fermenting regular cream with some kinds of lactic acid bacteria. The bacterial culture, introduced naturally or deliberately, sours, and thickens into cream, less is better. (This is my least favorite because they are pasteurized, all live bacteria are dead.)

16. **Sauerkraut**: Sauerkraut is a fermented food made from cabbage. Most of the bacteria in sauerkraut are *Lactobacillus* species. There are so many ways to use food to feed our guts. I sincerely hope you make a trip to an International Food Mart and try some of these fermented foods yourself. Many people groups daily gut health practice is to eat fermented food, especially if you desire healthy skin, hair, and nails, etc. The above are just a few known to me, all over the world, children are taught at an early age to ingest small amounts of fermented food. Some treat it as a delicacy.

Several L. acidophilus probiotic supplements are available, either on their own or in combination with other probiotics. Aim for a probiotic with at least <u>one billion CFUs per serving</u>. L. acidophilus can be taken as a probiotic supplement, but it's also found in high quantities in several fermented foods. It is a probiotic bacterium that's normally found in your intestines and crucial to health. Due to its ability to produce lactic acid and interact with your immune system, it may help prevent and treat symptoms of various diseases. In order to increase L. acidophilus in your intestines, eat fermented foods, including those listed above. by <u>Ruairi Robertson, PhD</u> on June 14, 2001

Generally, adding a couple of the fermented foods, together with overall balanced feeding, along with adequate hydration, sulfur rich foods include cruciferous vegetables like broccoli, radish and mustard greens, Tuna Omega 3 oils, zinc, iron, vitamin C and D, Flaxseed oil is a good source of essential fatty acids, almonds, sunflower seeds and Vitamin B, collagen, liver, egg yolks (especially home raised chickens with fresh eggs), the best source of choline, oysters and wheatgerm oil. All these quality nutrients will contribute to brain, tissue repairs to optimize your everyday wellness.

Wholefood, Synthetic and Fractionated Crystalline Vitamins:

There are three main categories of food supplements: Only one is a true real food supplement, the other two are vitamin supplements or organic nutrient supplements.

1. Food supplements: Taken directly from a food source, nothing is added or extracted from the synergistic micronutrients taken from raw food. (Only fiber and moisture are removed. Processed below 112-degree F to keep the enzymes active.)

2. Synthetic Vitamins (not a food supplement), sometimes labelled as crystalline vitamin molecule, produced in a lab constructed or synthesized mainly from non-food compounds such as coal tar (what they used to pave the highway), and primarily from corn sugar, the molecular formula of the organic nutrient is replicated. There are no co-factors which are vital for the body to utilize, especially when the body is in a deficient state, the absorbability and bioavailability are questionable. (Honestly, it may be producing very expensive urines.)

3. Crystalline Vitamins (not a food supplement): It has a food source, not classified as a synthetic vitamin. It has been exposed to high powered chemicals, solvents, heat, distilled, diluted, and

fractionated to the degree that the original foods are processed or eliminated. Therefore, it requires a higher concentration of the organic nutrient, increasing the milligram levels for market value.

According to the writings of Dr. Royal Lee (the Father of modern nutrition): Natural compounds are protein in nature, in the form of an enzyme or co-enzyme. Critical recombination with other members of the complex so it can function as a nutrient. <u>Natural complex</u> carries trace mineral activators, or the vitamin fails to perform, according to Dr. Lee, most if not all the crystalline component is lost through the kidneys. It can be detrimental to my health especially when I consider my body works hard for me to do all its functions. www.drroyallee.com

<u>Define dosage labels</u> on supplements: This is an oversimplified sample, how much and how often should be followed as listed on the labels. This very limited information as so many new products are bombarding the market these days. Please read the labels, each person is an individual. I suggest that if you are highly sensitive individual, or if you easily get upset stomach in higher doses, try a small dose. Never overdo it and be careful if you are on several medications. I have patients related to me that their physicians are advocating no vitamins. I am most empathetic because people are ingesting massive amounts of undigested vitamin tablets, much of them end up collected in the gut and the stomach unabsorbed.

- Serving size: This refers to the amount expressed in units in the form of capsules, tablets, or milliliters.
- Daily value (DV): A daily recommended amount in % based on a 2,000-calorie diet.

- Recommended daily intake (RDI): Recommended amount to be taken each day to maintain health.
- Directions: This provides specific instructions on how to, when to, and how often to take the supplement, some is best absorbed with food, before a meal, after a meal, just before bedtime, etc.

Flaxseed as Oil has high anti-inflammatory effects, and cold pressed Flaxseed Oil taken in raw form (non-heated) has great antioxidant properties. Flaxseed contains Omega-3 fatty acids and has high dietary fiber. Whole flaxseeds can be ground up into powder or flaxseed meal, but make sure you vacuum seal immediately since the powder can go rancid in hours. Also, if you get the bag of powder form, be certain you keep the bag in the freezer and keep checking if it turns rancid. The powder can be mixed into smoothies or used in pancakes or muffins recipes.

You can make homemade fruit roll-ups: by blending 1/2 cup of flaxseed meal with a ripped banana, strawberries or raspberries, place in mixer with 1/2 cup of water, add a tsp at a time of need to thin out the roll-up, once creamy and gelatinous, pour onto flat surface to place into dehydrator or dry breezy place to dry overnight. Makes a great sweet snack.

MTC Oil from Coconut: Choose the ones with no fill oils, this is a high nutrition dense food, great tasting and is good to add 1 teaspoon daily into your smoothie, due to the purity, taking a teaspoon daily is a good anti-inflammation measure.

Butter or Margarine:

The public lives by advertising, the "fat-free" culture has not benefitted our brain health. The brain needs fats, ghee, it's a lactose-free superfood alternative as butter alternative, it has high good cholesterol content, therefore use moderate amount as 1-2 table spoon for searing or sauté seafood or quality meat. I suggest 100% using butter, (and not margarine for fat as quality nutrient). Organic Coconut Oil, Olive Oil, Grapeseed Oil and Sesame Oil, a little will go a long way especially with sesame oil add drops for flavor but never use for deep frying, it has high anti-inflammation properties, for healthy cooking, never overheat the oil.

Mineral Salt or **Sea Salt** are best, we need salt, many people were told by western doctors to cut out salt to lose weight. But our body needs not the table salt which had been bleached and stripped of all mineral contents, but it does have added iodine. I certainly believe to rid the table salt in your dishes. But taking natural iodine as supplements. Do not skip salt entirely for long term, it's dangerous and you do so at your own perils, consult a nutritionist or dietician but let food be your medicine.

Sugar: The brain needs both fats and glucose, there are over 130 reasons to get rid of white table sugar for human consumptions. Watch out for HFCS-High Fructose Corn Syrup. it is in all processed or packaged foods and flavored drinks; it will be most challenging if you want to get rid of toxic waste. I mainly use Maple syrup, Raw local honey, Stevia, Date syrup, Monk fruit and Erythritol. Read the label for the sweetness equivalence because it is highly concentrated. You will want to start with about ¼ the amount that you were used to, test it first, most people do not like the taste because they use way too much, you will have the right taste to sweeten your coffee or any cooking. Your sugar craving may give you a fight at the start, try "one degree change" at a time. The packaged food industries do not have your health interest at heart. I occasionally demonstrated in cooking shows, and there will be fun zoom sharing, there are a lot of fun u-tube demos. Start gentle and not make too many suddenly changes.

Weight Loss

Whenever diet or nutrition are discussed, the question of weight loss inevitably arises. I'm confident that anyone who consistently follows the healthy eating lifestyle will experience as great or greater long-term success in weight control than that achieved by any weight loss regiment. The goal is not only to go by the number on your scale, but there are also various measures if you invest in a "Body Composition Monitor" a scale which measures by more than one number.

BMI: Body Mass Index is a number calculated from a person's weight and height, it registers a more reliable indicator of body fatness, although it does not directly measure body fat. BMI is used as a screening tool to identify possible weight issues for adults.

- Body fat is there surrounds and protect your internal organs. We generally carry two types of fat in our bodies. Essential fat and Stored fat.

- Essential fat, which is stored in small amounts for protection (example, in a case of sudden illness, it is essential that the body has adequate amount of quality fat to sustain day to day life functions)

- Stored fat, which is stored for energy during physical activity, also includes high intensity exercises especially competitive activities. Too much stored fat may be unhealthy. While too little fat can be just as unhealthy.

Also, the distribution of body fat in men and women is different, thus the classification of the body fat percentage is interpreted differently between the genders.

- <u>Visceral Fat</u>: Visceral fat is found in the abdomen and surrounding vital organs. It is different from the fat found directly beneath the skin, referred to as subcutaneous fat. Visceral fat can go largely unnoticed because it's not visible to the naked eye. Too much visceral fat is thought to be closely linked to increased levels of fat in the blood stream, leading to conditions such as high cholesterol, type 2 diabetes, and heart disease. Measurement of visceral fat levels are relative and not absolute values:
- < 9 is (Normal)
- 10< to <14 (High)
- Visceral Fat level >15 (Very High)

I strongly encourage you to stop pursuing the magical formula for weight loss, but be intentional to begin consistently following simple rules for healthy eating. I have observed repeatedly that many who lose weight too fast inevitably will regain back just as quickly. Therefore, the best goal to set is aiming to lose body fat by size measurements. (Size change matters more whenever I do a cleansing fast or detox protocol, fats on the back, waist and thigh areas are most noticeable.)

ACTIVTIES and EFFECTIVE EXERCISES

Hula Hooping

Even though hula hooping appears to be only done on your waist, it can become a full body workout. When you get good at it you can hoop from the chest, shoulders, hip, and arms as well. A study showed at the American Council on Exercise that just hooping at the waist can burn over 400 calories per hour. From another perspective, which is close to an hour tennis, hiking, or elliptical training. It can strengthen your heart muscle allowing it to pump more efficiently. Hooping can improve hand-eye coordination like riding a bike! Hula hooping can improve flexibility of your spine, hip, and muscle groups of the entire body. Waist hooping is rhythmic movement that is purposeful for the waist to move with back and forward or side-to-side movements. The movement from hooping can be a form of relaxation when it is easy to spend 30 minutes with your hula hoop, connecting your body and music while relaxing and de-stressing your mind. Hula hooping as a family brings lots of fun and laughter. When I first started hula hooping, our son in high school was rolling on the floor laughing, it's fun to laugh at yourself especially when this can be an inexpensive family activity! The key here is movement, not a sedentary lifestyle.

Regular hula hooping can help meet your exercise goals and provide aerobic activity, like dancing or swimming. On average women can burn 165 calories in 30 minutes, and men can burn about 200 calories in 30 minutes. There are also waist-weight hula hoops available at sporting goods stores and some fitness clubs. It must be fitted for US size reaching somewhere between your waist and mid chest when it is resting vertically on the ground. This is according to answer from Edward R. Laskowski, MD (at Mayo Clinic Marketplace health)

Rebounding

The concept behind the benefits of rebound exercise has to do with the action of acceleration and deceleration. These two actions combined with constant gravity create increased G-force (gravity force) felt by all your cells. According to research and writing, this oscillation of forces increases cell diffusion, flowing movement – in our bodies (water, oxygen, nutrients, hormones, enzymes) by at least three-fold. However, it appears most folks have them in their basement or garage. I strongly recommend you use it in the open air where fresh air circulates. Also, a stabilizer-bar is a must have to avoid falling. Rebounding is the most effective exercise and it's the least expensive piece of equipment to own. It is not restricted to weather or space; it requires only a total of 5-15 minutes a day. The benefits outweigh all excuses of sedentary habits.

While in Naturopathic College, I was re-introduced to the rebounder, and I am reminding myself of the most gentle and effective exercise there is. Rebounding relieves stress, stabilizes hip and sacrum muscles, and can reduce low back sciatica pain. It also promotes tissue repairs while releasing endorphins with much less chance of certain joint trauma or cartilage injuries of other strenuous exercises. Finally, it's the best movement for our bodies to detoxify the lymphatic system, all while increasing oxygen flow. The details and benefits of this activity are clearly explained by Albert Carter, sometimes named as the father of rebounding. Book entitled *The New Miracles of Rebound Exercise*

Gardening is an excellent activity. Try starting with an herb garden on your porch or inside on a windowsill. Caring for plants can do wonders to de-stress and for your own wellbeing. By interacting with flowers and flora mood and mental health can improve. Planting perennials is considered moderate intensity exercise. You can burn about 280 to 350 calories actively doing one hour of yard work or gardening, by planting, digging, and weeding during spring and summer. NYU's Langone's Rehabilitation's Horticulture Therapy manager, Gwenn Fried says "Nature has major impacts on health and wellness, we know that people's cortisol levels go down in a green calm environment." Some hospitals use planting and flower arranging as a type of rehabilitation for people recovering from injuries, surgeries, strokes, and other conditions. Just 30 minutes of moderate-level physical activity most days of the week can prevent and control high blood pressure, reported by The National Heart, Lung, and Blood Institute.

Growing your own food can help to eat healthier and develop a lasting habit. By eating an abundance of fresh fruits and vegetables, you and your children are more likely to try foods not eaten before. Spending time outdoors lets your skin be exposed to the sun, which prompts your body to get vitamin D, which helps your body to absorb calcium, a mineral essential for bone formation.

Gardening helps to reduce depression and anxiety symptoms. The act of growing plants helps boost your mood; it may have something to do with how it changes your outlook. You must have faith in your future. Growing something real, something alive, is a hopeful thing that you can do with your hands.

<u>My Gardening Story</u>: I had suffered a severe brain concussion almost 8 years ago. The headaches were like my brain was on fire. I was determined not to be stationary on my porch rocker, at times I literally had to hold on to my head with one hand, then water my basil plant with the other hand. Eventually, I was able to add Oregano, then Thyme and so on, soon I acquired some lemon plants which had no fruit the whole first two years, then only about 5-6 lemons the third year. But I kept going anyway, adding more garden herbs, and making my own fresh herb vinegar and herb oil. Eating well for health, I began designing what I had purposed as a retreat. Today, I am hosting retreat events, serving delicious enzymes rich meals. Never give up hope and keep your dreams alive, keep investing everyday one degree at a time every day towards your dream or purpose, I thank Ron McIntosh for his class and real understanding of "GRACE", I am living the lessons he taught.

This April 2019, my dear mother, my heroine graduated to heaven, not entirely expected! I can honestly say my garden has been a place of peace and solace, I was missing my families overseas, mingled with melt down tears on and off for over a years. This may sound so crazy, but I keep talking to my plants. From the first week of March to mid-June, I was flying back and forth for mom's hospitalization and then the memorial service in June, I was away, and my garden was rather neglected. It was even as though the avocado plant was in shock too. But by late summer of 2020, I counted almost 70 lemons and limes with an abundance of herbs, and the one avocado plant came back to life even though just for one season. My whole garden and green house heard me, they are alive. Everyday watching my garden grew harmonious to my process, even in the valley of "the shadow of death," hope arise!

I hope to get you excited about just beginning with something so very simple as planting some seeds, or a pot of Rosemary or Basil. Getting down and playing in the dirt, are my little piece of heaven. My husband scored big with me when he put in a greenhouse for my babies during the Georgia winters.

More fresh cooking herbs/and wellness benefits:

Sage was believed to improve memory, bestow wisdom, and long life. Great with meat, a perennial herb with a spicy, aromatic flavoring, both sweet and bitter. It is a relative of mint and very easy to grow. Supports lungs, liver, heart, kidney, and uterus. It's a muscle relaxant for nervous disorders. Sage may stimulate bile flow and is best combined with fatty meat dishes. Do not use sage as medicine. The best use is only in cooking. Contraindicated in pregnant women or history of epileptic seizures.

Rosemary is a perennial in mild climates. Often you can see it's used as a landscape plant and as an herb as well. The rosemary is a Mediterranean region native shrub. The most delicious Rosemary thrives near ocean mist. It's a warming herb that may help mediate conditions of cold, mucus, and dampness, as well as a potent antioxidant associated with slowing the aging process. It is recommended for folks with poor appetites. Rosemary stimulates the nervous system, is a wonderful brain and memory booster, and can increase blood flow to the brain. It's been suggested that adding several drops of rosemary essential oil right under the running faucet gives wonderful aroma and therapeutic value. Not advised as herbal remedy for pregnancy* If you pick Rosemary off from a shrub, you should always blanch in hot water for a few seconds (due to pesticides garden sprays). Rosemary is a potent antioxidant and can improve circulation like ginger does. A fun and practical idea is to keep a pot of Rosemary in a sunny window. I often brushed my hands over the aromatic plant and its fragrance is better than perfume.

Thyme is a warming herb that supports the lungs, spleen, kidney, respiratory infections, bronchitis, and whooping cough. Its flavonoids have been found to relax muscles in the trachea link to coughing and inflammation. Thyme is one the most popular all-purpose savory herbs for flavoring soups, stews, and sauces, it does well in slow cook dishes. It is valued in Greek culture, to burn thyme as incense.

Make my own <u>Honey-Thyme cough</u> drink:

2 Cups of very hot water + 2 Tablespoons of fresh Thyme, steep the Thyme for 10 minutes + 1/2 C. of Honey and add 2-3 Tablespoons of fresh Lemon juice.

This will stay fresh up to a month in the refrigerator.

<u>Stevia</u> is another herb. It can be a miniature shrub, you can grow for personal use, two or three Stevia leaves are enough to sweeten a cup of tea. It is a healthy herb that is thirty times sweeter than sugar and essentially noncaloric. The leave extract is used as an alternative sweetener and is a member of the daisy family. Stevia is the one sweetener people who suffer from candidiasis and yeast type conditions can tolerate. I have some in my greenhouse and I use the leaves for my Hibiscus Tea or just in lemon water.

<u>Ginger</u> as a medical herb, is very pungent and a spice native to Asia. It's also a medicinal herb that can be enjoyed fresh, dried, ground, or powdered in a wide range of dishes. Ginger is most famous for treating indigestion and nausea. Ginger can also act as a decongestant and has long been used to especially bring cold and heat in balances. It is anti-inflammatory, especially warming herbs for poor circulation, as well as arthritis pain. Ginger is found in almost all Chinese and Ayurvedic medicine. In any given Asian kitchen and restaurants, there will be daily fresh ginger root. Also, for longer shelf life keep the ginger stem or root in a dry cool place. When I find robust fresh ginger roots, I store them not in the refrigerator, but in a clean small bucket of sand where it will

stay fresh up to a whole month. Mixing a few drops of ginger juice in a gelatin mode can invigorate the appetite for people going through chemotherapy and helps with nausea. For a gallstone sufferer, it is advised not to overuse ginger, it is a potent while commonly used herb.

Especially during cold winter mornings, steep 4-5 slices (1/2" thick) of fresh ginger in large cup of hot water for 10 minutes, drinking by adding honey and lemon. After a week, you will find your joints and kneecaps warming up, especially if you take morning walks in the colder season.

Fresh Herb Arrangement on my kitchen counter and in my refrigerator. The best home use for food grade hydrogen peroxide is to keep cut flowers remaining fresh for a longer time. As well as keeping your herbs like parsley, cilantro, or green onions fresher longer (As soon as I return from the grocery store, I prepare a large mouth glass jar, then putting the herbs stems first, then fill the jar full of water, then add a ½ teaspoon of hydrogen peroxide giving it a stir). This preparation guarantees my herbs stay fresh in the fridge for as long as 10 days. I can pull out several stalks of parsley or cilantro as needed, doing so will prolong freshness especially for my organic herbs!

A cheerful heart makes good medicine, (Proverbs 17:22)

CHAPTER 3

DELICIOUS ENZYMES: ONE DEGREE CHANGE

What on earth are Enzymes?

What is often mentioned about but little is understood, enzymes are the catalysts of biochemical reactions in living organisms. They include the formations, the breakdown, and all kinds of rearranging of molecules all synergistically and harmoniously created.

For the sake of "nutrition," in simple explanation: The body makes and utilizes over 5,000 enzymes working hard like a team of traffic cops. There are mainly three major groups and many other subtypes working 24-7 in the body:

Proteases break down proteins

Lipases break down fats or lipids

Amylases break down carbohydrates

Food Enzymes are introduced to the body through fresh or raw foods. But over-cooking and processing of packaged foods, all the enzymes are destroyed. Therefore, your digestive system is working overtime. The best example is to take an apple, the enzymes at one time gave instructions and directed its biochemical reactions as an apple should, which are necessary for the growth of the apple will now become contributing food enzymes into your enzyme bank account to help the digestion of the apple in your stomach.

Therefore, consuming fresh, whole, and un-denatured foods, and in raw form, consuming fresh fruits and the fresh vegetables, which will activate an enzymatic access to all the organs, cells and tissues to utilize both body enzymes, and metabolic enzymes not just to sustain but thrive physically, but also to supply for many other activities, including cell detoxification and energy productions, etc.

A family legacy of eating enzyme rich plant base food: Once upon a time, our daughter in love was raised on American fast-food diets, since she joined our family she has incorporated eating for health. She currently eats for health so well and keeps the family healthier by eating plant-base food, I can verify that she is the energy bunny of our family and my grandchildren, they are good stewards of my "Delicious Enzymes" legacy. A family that eats together keeps together. The whole family are now mainly plant-based eaters, they are good home chefs, including the grandkids are healthy eaters, and they enjoy initiating being part of the salad prep team as pictured below, being creative adding apples and grapes to the salads:

One-degree Change-<u>Delicious Enzymes,</u> You may consider gradually try the following:

<u>Ginger Honey Morning Tea</u>

3-4 slices of fresh ginger root

1-2 tsp of raw honey

Hot (not boiling water) 6-8 oz.

(Great for circulation)

Breakfast Energy Drink (12oz)

1 large ripe banana

Half an apple

1 tbsp. flax seed powder

1-2 tsp Lecithin Granules (health food store)

1 Tbsp Nutritional yeast flakes

Handful of berries/grapes (or any frozen fruit)

Add 10 oz. of water and blend well.

> Superfood Cocktail found to kill 100 percent of the sampled breast cancer cells with no side effects.
> A 2013 study from LSU Health Sciences Center in New Orleans identified a super cocktail using 6 natural compounds.

Green Veggie Smoothie (lunch for 2)

2 whole tomato (remove skin-difficult for digestion)

1 C. fresh spinach

Half C. lentil sprouts (can use alfalfa sprouts)

Sm. amount of cilantro

1 Tsp. Dulse (seaweed flakes)

12-16 oz. water

Apple-Celery Juice (yields 4oz)

1 green apples

3-4 stalks of celery

Half a cucumber (include seeds)

Add half C. Water

Apple-Carrot Juice (for 2)

3-5 Carrots

1 green apple (to sweetened)

Add 1 C of Water

V8 Juice (Your very own V8 for 2/ use organic)

1 Apple

3 Carrots

1 zucchini

2 large stems of Bok Choy

1 large stem of kale (include stem)

1 tomato)

handful of spinach

1/4 C. Cilantro Leaves

Marinated Kale Leaf (3 stalks)

1 Tbsp fresh squeezed lemon juice

1 Tsp of sesame oil (for flavor)

Pinch of sea-salt

1 Tbsp of Honey, or

Pinch of Cayenne pepper

(Add to any fresh tossed salad)

Salad Dressing (Lemon/ Tahini)

1/4 C fresh lemon juice

1 Tbsp Tahini (or sesame paste)

1/4 C. maple syrup or agave nectar or honey

1 Tbsp Tamari or Fish sauce

1 tsp sea-salt

Pinch of cayenne pepper

1/4 C. of water

2 Tbsp of vegan mayonnaise

1 Tbsp of nutritional yeast (optional)

(Blend together can keep for 2 weeks in the fridge)

Salad (for 4-6)

1 sm. to medium stalk of Napa Cabbage (Asian sweet cabbage)

1 lgr. head of Romain lettuce

1 large stalk of Bok Choy (thinly sliced)

1 C. spinach leaves

2 large, sliced radishes

Half C of chopped red cabbage.

1-2 Roma diced tomatos

Granola (10 servings)

1/2 C wheat germ

1/2 C Raw almond

1 C. Raw oat

1/4 C. Pumpkin seed

1/4 C. Sunflower seed

1/3 C. Raisin

1/2 C. Flex seed powder

Try using Kefir milk (use non-dairy) or sprinkle on top of yogurt.

Porta bella Creamy on Zucchini Pasta (A cooked dish 4)

3 large porta bella (14-16 Baby Bella) Mushrooms (cubed)

1 large red sweet onion (can also add a yellow onion)

2 cloves garlic

2 stalks of green onion

(Brown above & gradually add water till half cooked then set aside)

2 Tbsp coconut oil

2 Tbsp tamari sauce

1 tsp sea-salt

2 Tbsp of vegan mayonnaise

Can add 3 Tbsp of lemon juice to taste (optional)

(Add above mixture to mushroom)

Pour over 3 Zucchini noodle (pasta or brown/9 Grain rice are options)

Brussels Sprouts with Almond flakes (2-3)

15 pcs. Brussels sprouts (cut into halves, about 30+ pcs steam till tender.)

1 Tbsp almond flakes

Pinch of sea-salt

2 tsp of vegan mayonnaise

(it's delicious using ½ Cup of the Creamy sauce above as well)

Chocolate Musse Desert (4)

1 large or 2-sm. ripe avocados

5-6 pitted dates (soaked overnight)

1/4 C. Cocoa powder

1-2 Tbsp agave nectar or Amber Maple Syrup

1 Tbsp water, add more in small amount until desired creaminess.

(Raspberry for garnish)

Raspberry Jam (1 C)

1 C fresh or frozen raspberries

1 tbsp of Chia seed (soaked at least 2 hr.)

2 tbsp of Raisins

1 tsp maple syrup

Spread on toast or as topping on plain yogurt

Broccoli-Cauliflower Salad (4)

1 sm. head cauliflower (or ½ of lgr. Head)

2 med. size broccoli crowns

1/2 tsp Cayenne Pepper

1 tsp garlic powder

1 tsp sea-salt

1 large tomato (dice/peel skin off)

1/2 red-bell pepper (chopped)

1 tbsp chili powder

2 green onions stalks (scallions)

1 tbsp cilantro leaves (chopped)

1 tbsp fresh basil leaves (chopped)

3 tbsp fresh lemon juice

1/4 C extra virgin olive oil

3 tbsp of raw honey

(Chopped the vegetables to desired small pieces)

Then fold in the herbs and spices in food processor)

EXPERIENCING "SMALL WINS" CAN GIVE US MORE CONFIDENCE IN OUR ABILITY TO KEEP SUCCEEDING

Food can affect Behavior: This is a serious concern for every parent, educators, caring health professionals and judicial branches of all governments:

Food & Behavior: *The Biochemistry of Crime* by Barbara Reed Stitt, Ph.D. (Print permission by publisher to copy parts)

Children given an average dose of food additives in a cookie showed significantly worsened behaviors. The study conducted by Dr. C. Kenneth Connors indicated that children given an average daily dose of food additives should be of vital interest to parents, and especially in the criminal justice system.

The actions of a person with toxic poisoning often become quite bizarre. I once had several probationers who had been arrested for indecent exposure. Their records indicated that they all worked at the same factory - they did a lot of work with metals. Subsequent hair and analysis revealed that all had acute lead poisoning. Although the connection between lead poisoning and these sorts of sexual misdemeanors is not well defined, stories like this led us to question whether the notorious flashers have dirty minds or simply poisoned ones.

A 19-year-old probationer of mine provides a classic case of how an undetected case of metal poisoning can ruin an entire life. The young woman had been arrested for shoplifting, but her problems started much earlier. she was classified as learning disabled as early as second grade and had a history of behavioral problems. Although she was strikingly beautiful, she saw herself as grotesque. She was a psychiatric mess.

She received a battery of tests at the Baron clinic, Illinois from which we learned she was extremely hypoglycemic and had toxic levels of lead and arsenic in her body. Biochemists believed that the highest concentration of lead the body can safely tolerate is 15 parts per million. This woman's lead levels were more than twice that -- 37 parts per million!

She was on a new dietary regiment and was given treatments to remove the toxins from her tissues. The woman was extremely uncooperative in the treatments, but still showed encouraging progress. After just a few treatments her lead levels were down to just 11 parts per million. In less than a year her I.Q. Scores increased about 30 points. She could drive again, continued her education, has stayed out of trouble and -- best of all -- she finally realized she is a very lovely person.

The depths to which metal poisoning can throw a person off, is illustrated in another case; This man was a Cleveland dock worker who had been arrested for a drug felony but managed to get off on probation for a lesser charge. I have seen a few human beings in worse physical conditions. When he came to my office, he was so weak he could not hold his head up. His hair looked like straw, and I found out he had been losing it by the handfuls for three months. He looked fatigued and uncoordinated. Analysis of his hair revealed that he had shockingly high aluminum levels --more than 300 parts per million. Suddenly his poor health and his criminal behavior no longer seemed a mystery to me. The wonder was that he could still walk!

I called the man and his wife into my office, and they sat opposite me holding hands as I told them the news: aluminum poisoning was contributing to his personality decay. In our conversation it developed that he had been working at an aluminum smelting plant for the past year, and he began noticing his physical and mental problems after getting the job. He and his wife broke into tears of happiness. The weight of guilt he had been carrying for months slid off. "You see honey," he sobbed to his wife, "I told you it wasn't me!"

So where do these toxic metals come from? Some from diet; foods stored in metal containers often picked up contaminations. One consumer digests study showed that most canned fruit juices contained high level of toxic metals especially dangerous are foods stored in lead dash soldered cans.

Drinking water can be another source of toxic materials, especially copper. Study of copper content of drinking waters in 27 locations in the eastern United States revealed that five were at or near the level of copper dangerous by the US public health service,

Other toxins: water that runs through lead pipes is often tested a source of lead poisoning. Cigarette smoking is a source of cadmium, lead and arsenic poisoning, soft drink dispensers, over-consumption of caffeine and its constant stimulating their adrenal glands.

It ought to be remembered that, in one sense, toxic levels of lead and other toxic metals in the body can be considered a deficiency disease. Absorption of many kinds of toxic metals can be prevented by sufficient intake of food sources: beans and apples, as well as quality nutrition. Furthermore, in many instances toxic metals can only masquerade as their nutrient counterparts when there is not enough of that nutrient present. Even though toxic metals in your body may be coming from the plant/factory down the street, how they affect you still depends on your daily diet.

Toxic metals: there are micronutrients; minerals also play an important role in the molecular processes. However, some metals are the most toxic. They are poisonous because they are antagonists to the beneficial minerals; that is that they take the place of nutrients in biochemical functions, thus ruining them. Zinc, for instance, is known to be extremely important in certain brain processes, and recent studies show it is beneficial in the treatment of schizophrenia. Lead, on the other hand, is a zinc antagonist. If there is too much lead and not enough zinc in the bloodstream, lead will take the place of zinc in neural chemical functions, with disastrous results.

This is not an exhaustive list of metal poisoning: Increase learning disabilities, increased hyperactivity, and even psychosis in some cases (Behavioral observation as a probation officer, Barbara Stitt).

Aluminum: speech disturbance, and coordination, paralysis, psychiatric disorders, and tremors.

Antimony: loss of appetite, dizziness, fatigue, headache, irritability, abnormal skin sensations, and nerve inflammation.

Arsenic: loss of smell dizziness, lethargy, abnormal skin sensations, peripheral nerve systemic disorders, nerve inflammation, and weakness.

Cadmium: fatigue, in ability to smell.

Lead: incoordination, convulsions, mental retardations, peripheral nervous systemic disorders, psychiatric symptoms, Tremors, visual disturbances, and weakness.

Mercury: appetite loss, speech defects, fatigue, headaches, incoordination, mental retardation, abnormal skin sensations, nervous systemic disorders, psychiatric symptoms, tremors, weakness, and visual disturbances.

<u>Tin:</u> speech impairment headache nerve inflammations, visual disturbances, and abnormal skin sensations.

I do have canned foods in my pantry for emergency reserves. However, I strongly suggest any can foods soaked in fluids, do not use the fruit juice and please soak it in salt water for 15 minutes then squeeze out any juice before serving.

I personally, even in a very healthy state, and rarely get flu or colds, Choose a lifestyle of periodic detox from one day, to one week, up to 10 days of cleansing yearly. The benefits of detoxing as well as occasional fasting combining spiritual and health purpose, I am responsible for supporting my own biochemistry as a living system consists of cells, tissues, glands, organs, etc. Allowing them to do a team function within, Enzymes in and toxic waste must go:

<u>Tissues:</u> includes skin, hair, nails, cartilage, fascia, blood vessels.

<u>Glands:</u> produces and extracts substances such as hormones, saliva, provided by the saliva gland, pancreas, and thyroid, etc.

<u>Organs:</u> perform functions for the heart, liver kidney, stomach, especially the complex metabolic process of filtering the blood.

MSG-Treated animals have in almost every case confirmed the delirious effects of high dose MSG treatment in the neonatal. MSG given to embryos and weanling rats causes marked inhibition of neurotransmitter activity as well as central nervous system damage. When rats received doses of MSG starting at the first few days after birth, they show less spontaneous cycle motor activity than controls and do significantly more poorly on certain kinds of behavioral tests.

Violence in America

General Americans people put into their bodies, for what we consume can easily induce violent and irrational behavior. Here are some thoughts that must be examined if we are to get a handle on violence in America.

1. A deficiency of B vitamins can create serious psychological disorders.
2. Many people with B vitamin deficiencies are being treated by psychiatrists when they are more in need of a nutritional supplement.
3. Many children eat a diet that is devoid of vitamin B and loaded with processed "non-foods" that induces a further depletion of vitamin B already stored in the body.
4. The "enriching" of processed foods with synthetic vitamin B fractions like thiamine does very little to resolve the B deficiency crisis in most people.
5. The single most common emotional symptom of vitamin B deficiency is a recurring feeling that something dreadful is about to happen.
6. Other emotional symptoms associated with vitamin B deficiency are:
   - Moods of depression
   - Insomnia
   - finding it harder and harder to cope
   - Chronic headaches and more on the horizon

Let us become more socially responsible about what is served in schools, health care facilities, jails, corporate cafeterias, and other institutions. Incorporating new nutrient rich Whole Foods and effective nutritional supplements into these settings.

Be sure to take special care in your own home as well. This is especially true if you have children. Taking B-complex Vitamins daily can help, especially when added to a good Whole food nutrient dense diet.

Many of the brilliant individuals whose ingenious works bring us such joy aesthetic and artistic satisfactions, these children are semi starved, emotionally unbalanced, and even suicidal human beings.

Besides the high sugar and nutrient depleted contents, processed foods provide a poor brain environment in yet many other ways -- they contain non-nutritive chemicals which may cause allergies or may be toxic. Every year, average person eats a total of about four pounds of additives: a huge dose of additive in any serving of food may be just a milligram or two as we said before, the cumulative effect of all these chemicals is simply not known. Who can predict the behavioral consequences of a lifetime of eating chemical congestions like the following?

Bleached flours, white sugar-sucrose (all calories), dextrose, corn syrup solids, shortenings along with antioxidant, leavening, nonfat dried milk, propylene Glycol monoesters, mono and diglycerides, wheat starch, glycerol, artificial vanilla flavorings, food dye/coloring, guar gum, citric acids, and artificial flavoring.

Detecting malnutrition:

Define malnutrition: A state of impaired functional ability or deficient structural integrity or development brought about by a discrepancy between the supply to the body tissue of essential nutrients, calories, and the biological demands for them. How to diagnose a case of malnutrition? How would you go about doing it? These are symptoms most associated with starvation:

Bloated belly, spindly arms and legs, dull eyes. Conception persists that malnutrition exists only among the poor and deprived nations. Suffering from malnutrition only when a person is literally on the verge of death.

Personally, and professionally, as a naturopathic N.D., I live most of what I preach. I am completely convinced a well-nourished body, and a well nurtured mind, are needed solutions to solve the mystery many societal problems of our time.

Sleep and Rest are so important, it's time for your body to rest and recuperate and restore vitality. Try to keep a regular rhythm to your sleep. Sleep is one of the most difficult conditions to pinpoint and to help people with insomnia (especially if they are on many medications). Everyone is different. Each carries emotions, lifestyle, grief, and stress. Called induced insomnia that is more prevalent than ever. When using Melatonin for sleep, in order not to wake up groggy, 2-3 mg. is good.

Also, I use medicinal herbs, with are the highly effective whole herbs liquid such as Valerian and Chamomile needs correct dosing. You can also try 1 Tbsp Raw honey and 1 Tsp organic Ceylon Cinnamon powder mixed with ¼ Cup of hot water (not boiling), it is most helpful occasionally. It is estimated 70% of Americans are Magnesium deficient, which contributes to general sleep issues. Picture below shows more on this little know mineral: by Dr. Barb Woegerer.

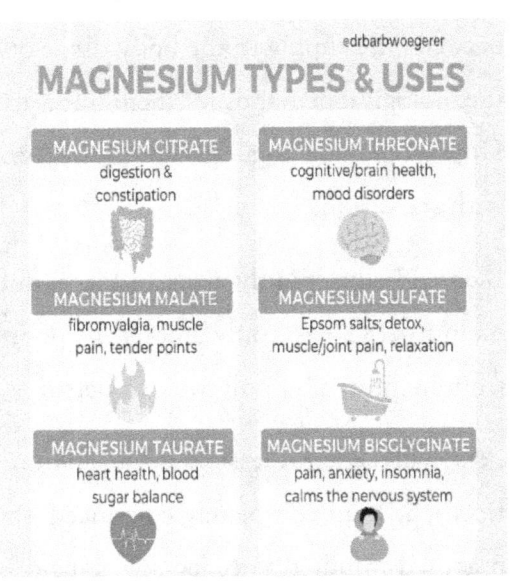

Please consult a professional who can evaluate many of the contraindications with your current health assessment, especially the prescription medications you are taking for symptom or disease management.

A Well Hydrated Body:

Reserves Osmosis is effective and adequate for an in-home water-filtering system. It is reasonable and easy to install for an in-home system.

Since our body weighs about 70% of water molecules. The brain itself is about 70% water. The blood is approximately 90-95% water and bone 25% water. On average, drinking half of your total body weight of water in ounces is adequate to satisfy your body's hydration needs.

Drinking an average recommendation of 7-8 (8 oz.) glasses of fresh water, provide for a well-hydrated body is crucial, drinking half your body weight in ounces or the recommendation of drinking at least eight glasses of water every day. Not to mention that a well-hydrated body is crucial to the skin especially if you care about youthful-looking skin. However, some studies that challenge the long-standing idea that over-drinking can cause water intoxication could potentially be fatal. The study showed that the brain activates a "swallowing inhibition" when excess liquid is consumed (or at too fast a speed).

In excess when forcing gallons of water is not a good sign. I do not have enough data to make further statements on over drinking water.

Average half your body weight in ounces of fresh water is adequate:

If you weigh 200 pounds, then 100 oz. of water is generally considered a well hydrated body: 10-12 (8 oz. glasses of water, not coffee, not soda, not fruit juices), if you are unable to drink that much water, consider adding a dash of mineral salt and steep in your water for your first morning 8 oz. remineralizers, such is good compliance when on most medications,

Acid/Alkalinity: <u>**Alkalinity is More Important**</u>

Alkaline refers to the pH of the water. Alkalinity refers to the water's ability to resist change in pH when acid is added. Alkalinity is necessary to neutralize the acid.

At the end of the day, it's not enough for water to simply be alkaline. Do be cautious when drinking "alkaline water over 8.7ph" for prolong period of time is questionable. Alkalinity is far more important because it doesn't only depend on pH levels. Bicarbonate neutralizes acids in the water, giving water higher alkalinity and making it the preferred form of hydration. According to Dr. Mark Sircus, OMD, DM, he stated that water treated with magnesium bicarbonate is the most beneficial. Using a reverse osmosis water system with magnesium bicarbonate restructures and neutralizes water to ensure your body gets the nutrient-rich, nature intended it deserves.

When you drink water that is high in alkalinity, blood can flow more easily throughout your body and guide oxygen and nutrients to your tissues. This, in turn, can improve circulation, increase hydration, regulate blood sugar, and enhance your internal system overall.

The pH Scale

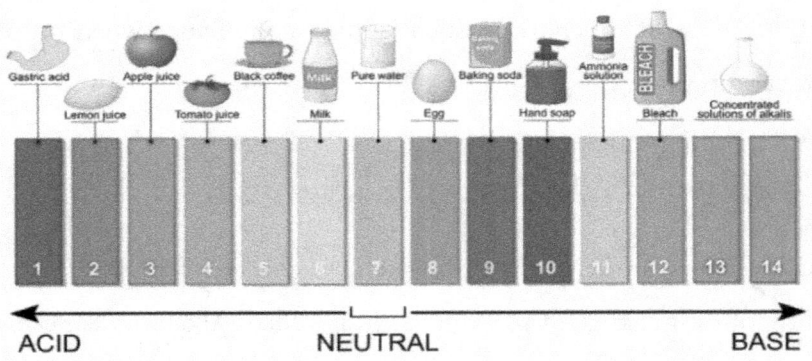

Beyond drinking clean water, you can also add Electrolyte drink mix. Especially when you are in a detox process. I keep my clients well hydrated at my facility, also advisable using any therapies anywhere: 1 tsp. electrolyte drink mixed with 8-10 oz. of water makes a big difference in your body pH and intake, keeping you well hydrated. Not to mention in any disease or surgical recovery process.

Check the labels before you get mail order or purchase at the health food store: Ingredients list should include Sodium chloride (salt), Potassium and Magnesium, <u>no added sugar</u>, no Gluten.

I recommend everyone to be cautious with many flavored sports drinks, most are sweetened with HFC (high Fructose Corn Syrup). Especially for those who work outdoors, children and teens in competitive sports, other athletes, and the elderly being cautious especially in extreme temperature. I carry packet sticks of electrolyte drink mix especially when I travel, on trains and planes. Listen to your body, do not wait till you are dehydrated. Children get dehydrated easily, they become too busy playing and they simply forget to drink. This is especially true in the Fall and winter seasons during outdoor play. Make sure they are hydrated well before and after outdoor time. They will appreciate drinking water (not soda!)

<u>A true story</u>: Wean little children from Sugar.

Many years ago, I was the assistant supervisor of a women/children Bible study, one half day weekly program: BSF (Bible Study Fellowship) in a mid-western town. It was a delight and an honor to serve the children from ages 2-6. It grew quickly from a few children to nearly a hundred of the most adorable children entrusted to the program and me. We tried our best to be congruent to the same study lessons the mothers learned from the development of the designated story theme, including proper snacks and drinks.

I handled a very small budget for snacks/drinks at break time because several teachers and I kept these children. There were very good intentioned moms that brought soda and colored fruit drinks at the beginning, but I had no place to store or keep the sugary drinks. The idea of heated car trunks carrying sugary liquids in plastic containers did not go well with me, according to my idea of refreshment not to mention sugary cookies these young moms furnished. At this time, even in the early 90's, there was little awareness of plastics toxicity and the impact of sugary fruit drinks. In those days, I did not have any professional trainings to justify my "healthy principles," therefore, I just politely turned every item away. Apparently somewhat disturbing to some young moms and other leaders, they legitimately questioned what exactly I was serving for snacks to their little ones. Each time, I responded with a simple but firmed reply of <u>water</u>, small loaves of bread or crackers or non-sugared cereal bites.

One curious mom who volunteered to assist us later confided to me that she was wondering how I managed to get her child to drink water, because at home or on outings, they simply have "cool-aide" or soda drinks. When I demonstrated my strategy, she was so relieved and did not feel guilty about removing sugary beverages.

My strategy was that halfway through the four hours planned curriculum, just before outdoor playtime, the children <u>watched us</u> empty paper cups and snacks. Immediately upon return they were ready with folded hands; it never failed that one would lead a short thank you prayer. Then they would eagerly get the snack and then we came around with a large pitcher of water. They are now so thirsty to drink fresh water, I can still remember their cute faces wanting more water and describing how delicious it was!

On occasions, the story of Jesus feeding with the loaves of bread, or Moses leading God's people out of Egypt, the children <u>watched us</u> sliced the bread in front of them. The snack is waiting while we led them to march around and imagine desert heats for a few minutes. Every time, it was amazing how pleasurable it was to serve the little ones. Indeed, I had a strategy and an agenda planned which was to implement less sugar, and to keep healthier routines. Indeed, more is caught than taught.

Water, adding lemon:

Daily adding ½ to 1 of fresh lemon juice to 8-24 ounces of pure water will assist in digestion as well as balancing salvia pH, especially after evening meals. (The juice from 2-3 organic lemons will stay fresh in your refrigerator for a whole week if stored in a glass bottle.) Should your dentist express concern regarding your teeth enamel due to acidity, you can assure them that you are drinking lemon water is for your health. If it is a concern of yours also, then you can rinse off your mouth with extra water. The goal is not to get all stressed out by getting into a debate.

Also, the use of fresh lime water can help those suffering from acidosis (body cells lack oxygen) which is an imbalance of Acid/Alkaline in the body cells. It may help/support the body to fight infections, fungi, etc. Lime is less acidic than lemon and can be an excellent support for an overworked liver as well. Drink by adding one tablespoon of fresh lime juice to a quart of purified water. This is very refreshing if you want added flavor to water.

Bitters and instead of antiacids: Our tongue is like the doorbell to the digestive system and tasting something bitter, as in bitter melons in Asian dishes, it has a cooling effect during the summer months when too much high stimulating heat, as in hot food is consumed. Taking in multi-enzyme supplement during a rich meal gives your digestive system a break when its already overworked in a toxic environment. It like the ringing doorbell to welcome in-coming food as well as waking up the digestive process by "turning on" the organs "Ding-dong! Time to eat, time to digest!" All the digestive organs' mechanism gets "turned on." They start to secrete digestive juices in preparation for the in-coming banquet of food! By tasting bitter on your tongue, you send a reflex signal through the vagus nerve directly to the liver, waking it up and stimulating bile synthesis in the gallbladder as well. If you are anticipating an upcoming festival meal, take some bitters-herb drops of one teaspoon mixed with 6-8 ounces of water. Occasionally, when meeting with friends for a rich meal, I would order a ginger ale or soda water with bitters instead. Also, Hibiscus or Lemon Bitters are popular at health food stores. People who constantly are chewing something like chewing gum may in fact be sabotaging their gut digestive function.

Chlorophyll or Chlorophyll liquid, the blood of the Green Plants. It has a green pigment, present in all green plants, it is responsible for the absorption of sunlight to provide energy for photosynthesis. It is high in antioxidants, beneficial for dry skin and may even reduce the skin pigment discolorations. It also boosts collagen production in the skin! In addition, chlorophyll is linked to some natural cancer prevention. It blocks carcinogenic effects within the body and possibly helps to protect DNA damage done by toxicity. In China, a randomized, placebo-controlled intervention trial involving 180 adults with a high risk of hepatocellular carcinoma and chronic hepatitis B infection gave participants either 100 milligrams of chlorophyllin or a placebo before meals three times daily. After 16 weeks of taking chlorophyllin, the trial study is suggesting chlorophyll indeed benefits liver health (my personal interview with People's Hospital inside China when we worked with the medical school).

Another way that chlorophyll improves detoxification is by speeding up waste elimination by bringing fluid balance and reducing occasional constipation. Preliminary research shows chlorophyll benefits metabolism and increases the likelihood of success with some weight-loss efforts. Other benefits are that it is helpful in lung function in high altitude traveling.

One structure of the chlorophyll is very similar to heme, which is a part of hemoglobin present in human blood. Heme, which makes blood appear bright red once exposed to oxygen, is bound to protein forming hemoglobin. Hemoglobin then carries oxygen to the lungs and via the respiratory system and releases it into the tissues throughout the body. Chlorophyll is considered beneficial to the immune system, considered a superfood, due to its strong antioxidant effect. While chlorophyll is totally natural, in the supplement form it is marketed as "liquid chlorophyll." As a supplement it is very concentrated dark green color; you may experience dark green stools indicating a need to reduce concentration. It can be very messy on clothing because it may permanently stain. Personally, I prefer the mint flavor. One tablespoon of Chlorophyll added to 8-10 ounces of water is a rich source of Vitamin K and A. You can purchase liquid Chlorophyll from your local health-food stores. These supplements have been in existence for more than 50 years and are safe to add to water with practically no side effects at all. An alternative to the liquid chlorophyll, is in capsule form which also can be found at your health food store. www.herbsetc.com High Chlorophyll Foods are Arugula, Endive, Green Beans, Leeks, Parsley, Spinach.

Liposomal Technology is gaining speed in the supplement world. There are benefits of Liposomal products in supplements that can be ingested orally or applied topically. It's designed for rapid uptake, optimal absorption, bioavailability and for longer circulation in the body as an effective nutrient delivery system. I often ingest liposomal Vitamin C especially when I travel to build immunity. (Sometimes in remote areas on overseas trips, I stock up some while in the U.S. they are sold in health food store in pouches).

Dermal Skin Health - Exfoliation before feeding topical Oil or lotions. There are many ways to exfoliate and remove the dead cells on the epidermis. "Skin rejuvenation" is simply a description for improving the skin from a physical and visible standpoint. Skin rejuvenation techniques help tighten, brighten, and firm up the skin by causing very mild and controlled minimum sunburn to specific areas such as the face, neck or décolleté. Such actions encourage a faster rate of cell turnover and may also stimulate collagen regrowth deep beneath the skin's surface. The general common procedures used in skin rejuvenation include lasers, chemical peels as well as micro-needling. There are highly effective ones from your local plastic surgeon's office. Having had years of experience in the aesthetic field. Several times I visited Tokyo, I experienced high-end technology at a Japanese skin-care research facility which broadened my horizons. Unless you are in the hands of well-trained aesthetic professionals, you can easily damage your skin. I have witnessed burns, serious injuries, trauma, as well as irreversible scarring. Post procedural after care are not optional for certain epidermis renewal. In 2019, I participated in a 9-month group beta study of micro-needling in home regiment, as my skin detected these controlled micro-workings of the upper dermis, it immediately responded by triggering the body's innate self-healing process. It will also activate replacement of the older upper epidermis layer of damaged skin with new, fresh skin cells. The rewards are time saving and visible improvements on my skin surface. The entire process takes 5-8 minutes twice a week for 2-3 weeks to see results. But accompany by a high UV block to the treated area post procedure is a must. Applying a quality sunscreen of 30+ every morning (sunny or cloudy) and may reapplying at mid-day on treated areas. Be gentle on your delicate face area. Please check into the science behind skin rejuvenation, this is an advanced yet inexpensive system. I have seen quickened collagen regeneration and skin cell turnover. It is more about removal of dead cells and exfoliating what we slathered on during the day, be sure to clean off all facial cosmetics before bed and maintain proper lipid and moisture balance. When a woman wears lots of products on their face, she is slathering lots of chemicals on. Be careful of "anti-aging" or "natural" on the labels, they are loaded with hormone disruptors. I worked with facial tissues a lot, also if over exfoliation, there can be irreversible damage to the upper dermal protections, and the skin can become tough and accelerates aging. Nightly proper removal of oil and water-soluble facial products and debris on the face, provides cell renewal creating a clean canvas to absorb quality moisturizer.

Recommended sunscreen for <u>facial</u> UV protections: SPF30 PA++ or SPF50+ PA++++ (PABA-FREE), colorless, too many choices these days. My personal choice of facial care products is manufactured in Japan. I had a history of post-partum cystic acnes, and Asian face can scar easily. PA rating on sunscreen labels, is for protection developed by Japan, each + sign is a higher ++++ grade of UVA ray's penetrations of protections, primary cause of skin aging and contribute to skin cancer.

<u>Dental Care:</u> If you are reading this book, I assume you are probably brushing your teeth twice daily, as well as flossing. Honestly, I do not do a good job at it, and I depend on my sweet hygienist's reminder. A cleaning every six months and yearly exam should be budgeted for the time and expenses.

I do have a homemade recipe for healthy clean breath, you may not totally replace your toothpaste, and continue to listen to your dentist while using common sense:

Homemade Fresh Breath Toothpaste:

2 Tbsp of Coconut Oil (organic Cold Pressed & Non-GMO)
4 Tbsp of Baking Soda
6-8 Drops of Peppermint Essential Oil
Stevia Drops (6 drops) or 1 Tsp of Monk Fruit (to desired sweetness)
In a bowl, use a fork to by hand whip all the above ingredients, in a few minutes the consistency should become creamy as the coconut oil softens then place in a glass container with a lid. Use a clean spatula to apply small amount in another smaller container conveniently by the toothbrush. The above recipe will be enough for at least 6-8 weeks. (Keep the rest refrigerated up to 3 months)

After a cold or flu season, it is wise to replace old toothbrushes. Changing toothbrushes every now and then is good health practice. Also, try sterilizing your toothbrush, by bringing water to boil in a pot, then remove from heat, place toothbrush to disinfect for oral hygiene. In doing this, you can be thoughtful for your family especially before Fall season.

Collagen: It is quite a popular supplement these days. It is referred as protein. I prefer Marine Collagen (Type 1 & Type II). Gelatin comes from Collagen. Collagen benefits are rich and multi-faceted, it includes reduction of cellulite or stretch marks. Its smooth gel-like structure acts like lubricant to the tendons, ligament, and swollen joints. In bone broth, the bones are loaded with collagen, when simmering in broth, the collagen gradually breaks down into gelatin. In ancient China, gelatin was one of the foods recognized for nutrition-medicine. Gelatin is great for food sensitivities, and it is widely used in repair of the GI tract. Additionally, Collagen improves skin and hair, as well as promoting healthy muscle growth. During workouts it boosts energy, and it helps tissue repair within the joints and arteries, it buffers the body from some of the effects of shock to the cartilage damage which may not show up till we get older. Collagen comes from Bovine (beef or cow, chicken bone), Egg Shell Membranes. You can make your own bone broth. Whenever I can, I get grass-fed cow bones from your local butchers, adding ½ a lime, ¼ to 1/2-inch width of ginger (lightly smashed). Add about 6 Cups of pure water, slow cook (for overnight) or use the popular "insta-pot" 20 minutes twice. You will yield a rich broth, or I call it Collagen Soup (add desired salt for taste).

Collagen Soup, another true story: As a child, my mother often cooked bone broth from fish or beef bones. My favorite memory was taking a trip to the fisherman's wholesale market. I lived on an island of beautiful Hong Kong where one side is surrounded by harbors, and the back side of the island covered with pockets of sandy beaches stretching to the South China Sea. Early morning on the western tip of the island were mainly fishing markets, full of fresh ocean marine, "the food moves, and fish will jump out of the open aquarium." They are freshly caught and usually not frozen. The sight and sound still rekindle thoughts of community.

At about 12-13 years old, my siblings and I took a tram on an outing. I was the leader of the pack; we were on a mission to the fish market. The sight, sound and smell of the ocean, salt water, and the scent of fresh meat just meant lots of activities for the merchants. We would ask for the large salt-water fish bones. (The size of these fish spinal cord measured approximately 6x4 inches, we could see the collagen gel within these bones, yah, those are the kind we like, never mind about fish part, we just could taste the steamy delicious broth). And I have never met a merchant who was not friendly to us kids, already know how to pick out the freshest spinal cords, restaurants have their chefs order these fish spinal cords for soup base. Once we got home, off we went to the kitchen to get the soup ritual started, which is always a family affair! It was a fond memory for me and my siblings. The bowl of yummy broth was heavenly not to mention the nutritional value! If you care to have beautiful nails, hair, and joints, I suggest Marine collagen. I am glad we are all discovering the true health benefits by being intentional about what we put inside our bodies.

Take Actions for Kitchen Hygiene. Since my mother was a nurse, she left us with the best kitchen hygiene practice! I keep a small container of gallon of water with 1 Tablespoon of bleach+1 Tablespoon of laundry detergent, this container of solution always occupies a corner of my kitchen sink. We only keep white dish clothes!

Recommendations: Every evening after dinner, the kitchen counter gets a good wipe down, let your sink get the same sanitizing wipe down as well, and the dish cloth, sink stopper or scouring pads immediately get soaked in the bleach/detergent solution overnight. Grimy dishcloths are the places where food bacteria thrive.

This small inconvenience has kept my two young children from many childhood ailments. My kids were spared from most after summer infectious disease even though it went rampart when children return to school. Please keep the bugs far from where you prepare your family meals.

Kitchen Hygiene: Changing one routine for a friend - A true story:

Once I was helping a young mother who was enduring a traumatic illness, with three young children about age 5, 7 and 15, and an overwhelmed husband. Her youngest was in the same nursery class as my little one.

I brought several home-cooked meals and some new white dish cloths; I thought I was thoughtful to bring along a special touch. I asked my friend where she keeps her clean dish cloth, so I can clear the sink full of overnight dishes. She pointed to the lip of the sink, hanging over it was a dark, wet dishcloth, she told me it's perfectly ok to go ahead and use the dirty dark smelly dish cloth because her children continuously use it. I gloved up, got some soap to rinse off the dish cloth. I realized it's already soggy, mildewed, and smelly. I was so glad I caught it. After cleaning, it was still dark but less smelly! To my bewilderment, the little boy came by to use the same dish cloth after his lunch, proceed to wipe his hands without washing, and then his nose with it. I then realized it was placed most conveniently by the lip of the sink.

I asked if my friend would not mind if I replaced it with what I brought. My friend gave me a thankful sigh of relief but then she asked, "why white and how does color relate to good old dish cloth?" I was so glad she asked, and I am thankful she didn't take it personally after I explained that it's good housekeeping habit that my mother taught me (who was a nurse in Thailand's birth center). My mother had passed down some rather strict household hygiene disciplines to me. One being that any light color should help to see the dirt buildup. Especially where young children get frequent flu and colds, going around re-infecting the whole family, which is not uncommon.

<u>More Thoughts on Kitchen Hygiene,</u> many of us purchase organic vegetables or spring mix, notice on the box that is been twice washed. I would recommend you rinse off when you are ready to prepare your salads. Consider the traveling journey of your fresh or organic vegetables.

- Time from harvest to the wholesaler:
- Time from wholesale markets to processing plant.
- Time from process to the warehouse.
- Time it takes for travel to various regions.
- Time the vegetables sit on your grocery store refrigerator shelf.
- Time it took between your trip (warm car ride) from the grocery store to your refrigerator.
- Time between you in your refrigerator meal preparation (mindful of how long it's been there)
- Lastly getting it into your digestive tract.

Not many people will agree with this but rinse it off before the veggies go on your plate, due to oxidation you may notice some of these beautiful vegetables may be hidden with pieces of greens that have been wilted. Therefore, as you prepare your salad, do your best to rinse off and discard those broken pieces vegetables that already have been wilted and to avoid foodborne bacteria. Such occasions necessitate recalls from contamination of salmonella we all heard about.

Dr. Lila, PhD: Post-harvest handling of the berries, for example, the amount of time between picking in the field and your plate has a huge impact on the levels of photoactive compounds. Is to have that berry picked in the field and quick-frozen right there, close to the field, like they do for wild blueberries and buy them frozen because that is going to have everything in it. Those same blueberries in a fresh clam shell in the produce isle that may have been sitting there for several days are not going to have anything close to the photoactive compounds of the frozen berry that was frozen that same day. It's just how it is. Dr. Mary Ann Lila, PhD, Director of North Carolina State University's Plants for Human Health Institute. Health enhancing compounds in fruits, vegetables, and herbs, isolating phytochemicals that counteract malaria. (Altern Ther Health Med. 2018; 24 (S1: 28-29.)

CHAPTER 4

STRESSED ADRENALS

Stress -Human stressors

Stress - The Internal Dumpster

In general, much of the stress we encounter can be dealt with by prioritizing regardless of importance; We can easily inflict worry and frustration on ourselves, but we can also easily eliminate stress and worry and the feeling of being overwhelmed. Indeed, there are false responsibilities that seem real, depending on your unique personality type.

Choose Daily Can Do and Can't Do Concerns

Let's start with daily we can jot down items that we can do and items that we can't do. We can do our laundry and we can take the car for oil-change. We can conserve energy by turning the thermostat up and down. and we can water our garden and we can control our work and rest schedules. However, the things that we can't do are to manage other people, their opinion, personalities, dysfunctions, and their choices which can be overwhelming. Our co-workers' attitudes, political remarks,

social media, blogs, and network opinions are a paramount source of stress these days. Recent social and broadcast events no doubt can become major stressors. The urgent messages sent from very well-meaning families, friends, and co-workers

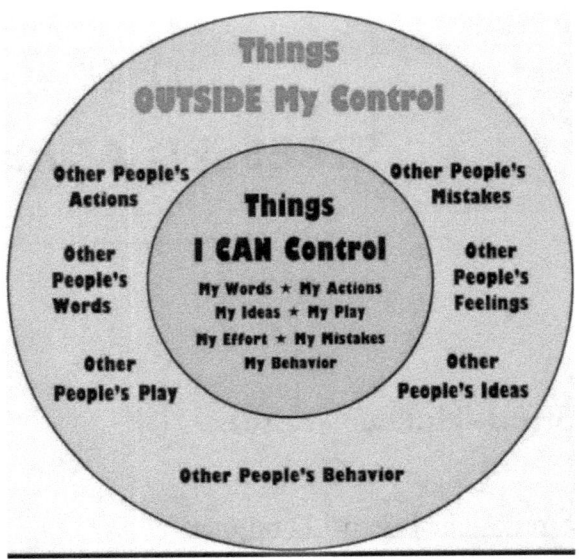

throughout the day. Too many times when I checked on the validity of these "urgent messages," I learned some outdated information continuously being recirculated, its value already deemed obsolete!!

Most stress we experience is a direct result of numerable urgent demands upon our time and our emotions regardless of their importance are very easily become distracted. For instance, a box full of email is better to accomplish the important task and subsequently respond to messages on the email than to accept all interruptions that come your way 24 hours.

President Dwight D Eisenhower who used <u>The Priority Matrix</u> extensively is often quoted as saying what is important is seldom urgent and what is urgent is seldom important. It's also believed that the concept was passed down to him by his mentor. The use of priority Matrix was later made very popular by author Stephen Covey.

What Stress does to Your Adrenal Glands:

There are two parts to our adrenal glands. The inner part called the medulla which is responsible for producing and releasing chemicals responses to threats, which we call the fight and flight response hormones. Such reactions cause elevation of heart rate, a rise in blood pressure and cause the pupils to dilate.

The adrenal cortex also produces cortisol or cortisone. They are best known to help maintain blood pressure and even regulate the breakdown of fats, carbohydrates, and protein. And it blocks the immune system's inflammatory response to injury cortisol also taxing to maintain the body's response to stress. Now the stress response is meant to be a short-term design, with the expectation that one or two things will happen quickly, fear will be successful eliminated, or death will occur along shutdown of non-critical bodily function is either expected or intended.

I observed many people routinely find themselves under constant, unmanaged stress. If such distress is not addressed regularly by the message presented earlier in this. It will become chronic and adversely affect adrenal activity. you will reach a point in which adrenaline and noradrenaline no longer require the simple fight or flight, but to keep running, and you keep going. Cortisol will remain elevated to keep on top of the perceived stress or threat.

We recognize two diseases caused by adrenal dysfunction; Cushing's syndrome is caused by sustained levels of abnormally High cortisol. It is characterized by body weight gain thinning of skin easily bruising loss of bone strength, fatigue, hypertension, diabetes, loss of sex drive, increased irritability, anxiety as well as depression.

Then adrenal failure, which is called Addison's disease, is characterized by chronic fatigue, muscle weakness, weight loss, low blood pressure, irritability, depression, craving for salty food due to increased salt loss, irregular Menses, and hypoglycemic which is low blood sugar. (I personally suffered from adrenal failure during a period of extreme challenges) I had to give myself the gift of rest as well as identify the stressors in my life.

Finally, there is adrenal fatigue, it's not characterized by abnormally High cortisol level, nor is it characterized by the extremely low hormonal level like the Edison disease, adrenal fatigue is the state in which the adrenal gland has become unable to keep up with the demands placed upon them in a chronic state. The body is now at the risk of other disease or symptoms development I simply remind my clients; your body has been borrowing from "Peter to pay Paul." Chronic stressed mental and emotions can translate into the biological age of the body as premature aging as well. The most common form of adrenal fatigue is exhaustion, failing to awaken or refresh after a full night's sleep and referred to as brain fog or cloudy thinking. Adrenal fatigue often goes unrecognized. For my work in nutritional counseling, I conduct a stress survey to help identify the daily stress level people are experiencing. Some people must take naps to simply get through their daily regular routine. Be kind to yourself so you can extend kindness to others! Get help, hire help, receive help when you really need to recover.

Adrenal fatigue can occur when the body requires adrenal hormones to sustain a stress response for a prolonged period. Regular quality foods and nutrition are required for hormone production. Oftentimes is the combination of both when the adrenals are off, they overworked and unreplenished. If normal adrenal function is to be restored, two things must be considered:

1. The demands placed upon the glands must be decreased.
2. And the resources available to them must be increased.

Doing one without the other is unlikely to resolve the stress challenge. My work is to help folks to understand where they are. And to consider ways to use quality nutritious food and wholefood supplements to balance the deficit, bringing awareness as well as inviting them to take steps to build towards wellness may take 3-12 months. I often see dramatic responses (within hours sometimes to a couple of days which really can be so exciting to see) with proper supplementation.

Breathe, by definition, breathing is the process of moving air into and out of the lungs to facilitate gas exchange with the internal environment, mostly by bringing in oxygen and flushing out carbon dioxide. We use oxygen to break down food for energy and produce carbon dioxide as a waste product. Breathing provides a mechanism for speech, laughter and similar expressions of the emotions. It is also used for reflexes such as yawning, coughing and sneezing, interestingly all involves breath.

We rarely think about how we breathe, Until I had an accident, my life was nearly taken away within seconds, with seven broken ribs, I literally was unable to move without excruciating pain, needing three months of high dose pain medication, oxycodone.

I am thankful, that when in such horrific pain, these drugs are available not just to ease pain but to force myself to breathe with an oxygen meter. The trauma team was very serious about reminding me to breathe deeply, throughout the day, regardless of how much pain I had to endure. Due to infection to the lung or pneumonia is a major concern of the doctors. During my recovery, I was very intentional about re-learning how to breathe again.

This is not the only way nor is the best way, but I believe the exercise was very beneficial. Even though it is very simple, it was vital to keep from lung infection, it can correct posture and strengthen the diaphragm and surrounding muscles, while supplying the necessary oxygen. Doing so will also bring a feeling of calm and restfulness, before and during stressful moments, remind yourself to breathe, any airway obstructions will short circuit your brain and gut function optimally.

1. Blow out long continuously through the mouth, clearing the lungs.
2. With lips closed, inhale through the nose as though smelling something pleasant, holding and counting to eight, while keeping hands on your chest or stomach.
3. Then exhale by making a whooshing sound through the mouth, holding, and counting up to 8.
4. Repeat 3 or 4 times and eventually work up to eight repetitions.

I also look up the word "spirit" comes from the Latin *spiritus*, meaning breath. Historically, breath has often been considered in terms of the concept of life force. The Hebrew Bible refers to God breathing the breath of life into dirt to make Adam a living soul (nephesh). It also refers to the breath as returning to God when a mortal dies.

"MONTH SITTING: WHAT IS THIS? (A revival trend for new mothers)

Rest may include sleep but there is so much more to rest. Imagine how a whole month's rest in the Chinese tradition. When I was a young mother, I was so excited to show off my baby, it was a mistake. Being in the middle of December, I took only about 3 weeks off and went right back to work, though I started only on half days the first week (I just wanted everyone to meet my new baby). But I did not recover well, I ended up with a bad case of the cold, then another cold, I didn't have any help while my husband was in first year of medical school. We had no money, but lots of love. I was all thumbs, a nurse friend came to help with breast feeding, she was a God sent. I wish I had planned well and surrounded myself with a caring community so I can be better restored. I am including the following Asian practice to remind us, there is a place for independence, however, its healthy and appropriate to receive help and be celebrated by accepting focused help. Postpartum moms must be wise to ask for help, plan and pay someone because you need it. The following is now becoming trendier and a more well received idea.

For the precious postpartum mothers: this tradition is certainly the best idea. I hope Westerners will catch on to the practical benefits of the best example of rest in other cultures. This is the ultimate practice of receiving the gift of pampered attention for a full month. It may not immediately appeal to everyone, but if you consider the long-term quality of life, it's worth trying!

The tradition is called "Month Sitting," and the practice dates to the Han Dynasty more than a thousand years. It was meant for the royalties but caught on by most of the upper middle class throughout Asia, but also similar practices around the world.

Immediately after childbirth, it is crucial for the health of the mother to be cared for and restored. Being many families were from farming communities, with mother, mother-in-law, cousins, and siblings. It has been an ingrained culture requiring adherence from the new couples too.

The new mother's only assignment is to focus on her rest and recovery, bonding with her child is a significant time as well. The "Month Sitting" concept was rooted in ancient Chinese therapeutic medicine. A holistic doctor simply reminded the in laws with strict compliance. Cold and wind are considered pathogenic factors, meaning they may trigger a disease process, as weather and temperature can affect the baby and mother's immune system.

Bundling up is always a must even while indoors, also avoid going outside. Shower nor tub bath are avoided as the cooldown afterwards could be associated with getting chilled. Childbirth is a very depleting process in a new mother's life, often accompanied with a fair amount of blood loss. In Chinese medicine theory, certain foods can help replenish the energy flow "qi" in the blood. In the West, we call it circulation.

Cold raw foods are not desirable in most Asian cuisine, considered most likely to carry bacteria. Usually when the bride married up socially, it was a sign of honor for a new mom to be receptive to her mother-in-law's commanding gesture insisting a whole month of undisturbed rest. Her side of the family, only the mother can make brief visits. It's a sign of trust her daughter is well cared for, the newborn stays only with the mom. The new mother will get to feast on Bone Broths (mainly chicken or fish bone broth), cooked ginger and eggs in malted vinegar (to bring warmth to the body). Figs, Dates, and berries all must be served at room-temperature. Steam greens and very colorful seasonal vegetables. Only rest, eat, sleep, nursing, and bonding well, the two don't go anywhere, the new dad visits during the day (as breast-feeding is a norm). Sometimes, the new dad sleeps in another bed, if the mother and baby are not sleeping through the night. No other distractions, especially no visitors because people bring germs and infections, the concept was excited visitors can bring stress and interfere with breast feeding, such as social gossips, unwanted advice and inconsiderate comments are intercepted. The mother is to use this time of rest, to plan and prioritize her recovery, potentially preventing postpartum depression, preventing future health deficits. All the while promoting healthy immune system and milk production.

When the 30 days pass, the new mother will be introducing the new baby to everyone, depending on the size of the family and extended family guests.

There will be joint efforts to organize a 10-course banquet to celebrate the month sitting is officially successfully completed. Signifying both mother and baby are well cared for, now both are ready to greet the guests. This was rather a status symbol for the father's side of the family. Also, to ensure that the mother's own family can be at peace, that their daughter has been well pampered as well as recovered adequately.

It is now becoming an industry involving luxury hotels with mid-wife service lived in. A day nurse in the room for most of the month. Now a modern status symbol in big cities in China, and under the self-care self-nurturing or motherhood industries.

CHAPTER 5

GOOD GRIEFS AND BRAVE HEARTS

———◆———

I am often reminded of the song "People need the Lord" encouraging you to be bold to share it whether it's at a store, on the job, or to the neighbor. Smiles are always good to start to initial interactions, several instances boldly but lovingly, I practice compassion without compromise of healing insights when needed.

Most of my clients feel freedom and safety in discussing any topic that is causing negative aspects in their life without the fear of being judged. Compassion and acceptance are the main ingredients in building trust. Being able to learn a little about where they have been enables you to see that some are simply exhausted from living life; misunderstood and not heard. Also, my listening allows them to provide proper information I need, and to know what steps I can offer to help or refer to specific experts.

Generally, the mindset and expectations are based on what most westerners believe. Some don't expect to be heard and therefore I have open-ended questions to hear their opinions. Where it gets challenging is when they want immediate relief. Some have a need to tell me what they already know from the internet. Although gathering information can be a very responsible action, but self-diagnosis can be frightfully costly.

<u>Fear</u> Complicating Symptoms:

One young man comes to mind about fear complicating symptoms. As a pilot, he was not able to exercise or attend to his work. The bottom of one foot was experiencing sharp pain. He was unable to explain adequately the frequency and intensity of pain as it was so irregular that he limped one minute and then walked normally the next. I observed that he was accurate in his description, but he realized that he'd have to prepare to face the harsh reality of irreversible disability. The fear coupled with the imagined loss of career was almost tearing him up. He was not willing to alert the insurance company to file for treatment protocol!

He had partnered with a massive dose of fear. He was quite convinced that the Google diagnosis was describing the very details of his symptoms. I waited until he finished talking, when I shared my thoughts. He was not only relieved, but consented to my suggestions, perhaps it was because his mother sent him my way. I didn't make any promises, but offered him a couple of options, since he already suffered over six months. Also, I reassured him that he will be referred to a specialist after a couple of days. He became so pleasant and engaging, and his countenance was more relaxed, because for 15 minutes he was trying to convince me to search for details to confirm his own diagnosis. After three appointments in 48 hours, he was pain-free, and he was very cooperative with what I shared. Three years later, he reported back that he remained pain free, and forgot all about his months of fear and worries!

Extreme toxicity: A woman came to me, complaining of headaches after she slipped and fell and as s a result, she had to quit working. She did not go to a doctor, had no X-rays and no medical records. I explained that I help people by utilizing detox and muscle tests, to decongest the gut and especially to influence them to take responsive measures towards holistic health. She filled out all the preliminaries and reiterated her desire to go "all natural." I agreed to meet her for two visits to see if she would gain improvement with some supplements after needed tests were done.

Additional complaints revealed that she had more symptoms from brain fog, sleep issues, digestion as well as weight issues plus a host of others that were all unrelated. In addition, she had a very difficult backstory. Again, I explained what I do, and in her case, she needed an orthopedic doctor ASAP for a lower back injury. She returned after 2 weeks when I discovered she didn't want supplements in capsules or pill forms. On the second visit she shared overwhelming stresses at home and obvious discomforts. I was more focused to gain clarity with honest feedback from her as to what her real needs are ?!

Finally, my conscious concern was to present her with truth not every woman is always willing to face! I asked a direct question about when she had her bi-lateral breast implants. She said that it was a long time ago, and she revealed that one side of her implants had migrated. She thought it was unimportant to our visits as I am not in plastic surgery. (she's unaware of my work history.) I had some suspicions of chemical toxic overload, but being in the cold season, it's not easily detectable. However, I knew there are more gut toxicity issues also. I am not convinced I could help her!

After 15 minutes, I need her to answer very specific questions: When did you have your <u>breast implant</u> and <u>what brand</u>?? Initially she was hesitant, but she answered somewhat defiantly inferring that my not being in plastic surgery would make me "unqualified" to expect an answer. She continued to insist on wanting more detox therapies. I sat her down and explained that I am concerned enough that she must accept my referral, I then handed her a female plastic surgeon's name which I already researched who specialized in removal of the old implants.

Since 2009, the breast implant community globally discovered BII (Breast Implant Illness). If someone has had such a procedure, the implant recipient is responsible for prophylactically keeping records of the foreign objects in their bodies, in the event someone's breast implant had migrated or leaked, which was my patient's case. No wonder she was literally acting crazy with the body circulating toxic blood, along with too many unexplained progressive chronic symptoms, pain, anxiety, and more. I was so thankful that she took immediate actions to get explant surgery, she was most fortunate that it turned out very successful. She later jokingly shared with me that I forced her to seek permanent resolution and that I saved her life! If you are having unexplained immunological responses and no answers, find out more below:

https://www.chrisbeatcancer.com/dr-kevin-brenner-on-breast-implant-illness-cancer-and-explant-surgery/

What about tears? Do I really need to grieve?

The topic of tears: it is to decongest the emotions inside. Tears serve to decongest the thoughts. I often asked patients if they could scream or cry. I pose such a question because sometimes that is when I find someone who's been very oppressed. From incest to rape and other traumatic events, some people literally cannot scream even if they are in an urgent situation. Truly taking time to grieve is a healthy and powerful way to be restored. It is an honest and courageous act. I noticed some people can't cry. Once I asked a grandmother, a patient of mine, if she could cry. She remarked that crying was not part of her. I gently pressed a little and she said she couldn't cry. Her eyes looked rather distanced. Her daughter who brought her in confided that her mother is a strong woman and she had not seen her mother cry. I asked her if she knew why. I must credit mother and daughter for being honest with me. Later, I learned she had an awful lot of fearful experiences where she had learned to shut down her emotions. Not only that, during the initial visit when she was brought in by her daughter, she refused to have eye contact with me. So much anger and harshness she had endured in her life. She had difficulty answering my questions. But I was surprised at her follow-up visit when she brought me a pound of fresh picked blueberries. Not only that, but the daughter also reported that during worship time at her church, her mother went up to the front of the church and danced. Finally, about a year before her death, she told me she has not known how to have a good cry!

Tears are another way of detoxing from emotions of past hurts. Crying may be one of your best mechanisms to self-soothe and be comforted. Crying also activates the parasympathetic nervous system (PNS). It helps your body to rest and digest. It shows your strength. Showing and sharing your emotions by letting out tears in front of someone takes a very strong person. Sometimes if we're not experiencing intense emotions or having meaningful space to genuinely express being upset, our body may not produce tears. Crying is often a response to strong emotions, such as sadness, grief, or joy. The inability to cry can have numerous possible causes; depression, trauma, personality factors, social stigma including cultural, and customs implied that crying and letting out tears are not necessary or considered unbecoming.

Some people just laughed off the intense emotions, especially if they had a history of being labeled by others as inappropriate, or from an overly refined family background. Such remarks were lies used to shame the previous generations and cynical or sarcastic statements to withhold tears from self or others.

Sometime a critical nature is camouflaged —not readily evident to most people. Such characteristics are very powerlessness, which are the classic traits of an orphan heart:

- Concealing personal hurts and may have hidden fear of abandonment.
- A sense of Power can be obtained by a controlling demeanor to obtaining revenge from previous offenses to even the score (its not even the same person, setting, context or season).

- Slander and put-downs to hurt others to feel superior and significant.

I have a couple of experiences of good griefs and cleansing tears:

During a very intense period in my marriage, Pride blinds, lying and deceptive associations were exposed right before my eyes. While I stood for truth and protected my family from innuendos/drama within a small community, I was the target and censure of jealousy and betrayals. This included involving finance, power, and thieves on the executive's level. Some folks simply cannot celebrate others' success. The malignments came from several sources. And the in-laws come rushing in adding insults to injury. The stress had caused me a great loss of appetite and subsequently I was down to barely ninety pounds. I found myself in a very manipulated environment (weaving in between, I knew I was known by God, and my Father was there the whole way!)

Being exhausted, with no help, I didn't know if I should check myself into a hotel or a hospital, but I was aware that I needed a place of safety and rest to get help to debrief from a congested soul. God is very faithful. I was very aware of the walk through of a complex difficult trial. I keep praying the Word and enough sense to get help is an asset. It was His grace and being honest to say I must get help. I am waiting for just the right door to open, which is not a passive lifestyle. It's like getting on an airplane: The stewardess announces to parents that in the event of an emergency, parents must take the oxygen first before helping a child.

Asking for help from wise people, you will know who your real friends are. Since I served many people in my community and volunteered much. I know myself well enough that when I am in pain, I have nothing to give. <u>Whole people gather and hurt people scatters</u>. The oppressiveness lasted almost 3 years. Later I joined a cosmetic dental clinic at another city. One time when my boss and his wife returned from a week off. Their countenance was markedly different than when they left, looking bright and refreshed. I boldly inquired about their visible difference. They shared about what they received. They thought I would benefit from it too!

I went and soaked up some practical truth with anointed teachings. As I sat through each session, I showed up and I received. As I journal and began to realize the heaviness was starting to lift. The next teaching was on oppression and grief. I will never forget what came next was an activity that needed very clear explanations, so I went ahead and stood up. The facilitator then instructed a few gentlemen, pastors, and fathers to stand with each woman, one on one, and publicly release a father's paternal strong arms giving each woman a fatherly hug. Many women had not experienced safety around men, no less receiving a fatherly hug and blessing. They were available for the women to weep and sob on a fatherly shoulder. Oddly, a young man came standing facing me. Quietly I wondered why did he come forward for me? He realized that I could be his mother as he said he was just twenty. I asked for his name. When he told me, I went limp, and tears started streaming as I laid my head on his shoulder. He had the same name as my son. God ordained the moment for a rapid release, and the dam broke. God knew the acute degree I had missed my children. I really couldn't weep or cry for over 2 years prior to that moment. Within seconds, a blood curdling loud scream came out like a heavy freight train, bellowing out of me from my chest through my head and through my vocal cords. Instantly I knew my voice and emotions were close to shutting down. I felt a peace that really passed all human comprehension. When God encounters us, the scenery may not look very dignified, but this is truth with everything right. I was able to cry thereafter. There had been a war on women's voice (including men and children these days) and now I have my liquid tears of gold.

When you can cry for emotional reasons, those tears contain stress hormones that help relieve the body of stress-induced chemicals. It's a way to decongest to help as you are quite literally shedding stress. Holding in emotions can be hard on physical and emotional wellness. Mental health is greatly affected when you repress your emotions. Bottling up negative emotions like anxiety and anger can disrupt the normal functions of your stress hormones, called cortisol. This can have lasting results in lowered immune function and an increased risk of developing a chronic dis-ease.

Another occasion was when my own mother finally passed after a most successful surgery, but no post-surgical wound recovery. She suffered from hospital sepsis, and the abdominal wall did not close completely to complete the recovery. For the following whole year, I was generous to my own heart to allow for timely and untimely tears, I would give a gentle warning to folks around me: "my tsunami tears are coming!" Sure enough, after about 3 minutes, it would be sunshine, it was healing from whatever wells up and the heaviness would leave. I was taught some healthy lessons regarding grief, to allow the emotions to be freed up and not hinder the flow of tears, especially from missing loved ones like a parent. This too is a part of being whole. <u>I must clarify that I am not a grief counselor.</u> There is absolutely a need for quality counseling, and I encourage you to be real with yourself. It's true we can't give something you don't have, healing is the children's manna.

The Word of God says: Yea, though I walk through the <u>valley of the shadow of death</u>. I will fear no evil. Psalm 23:4 (NJK).

It's a walk through in fulfilling the completion of life on earth in relations with my mom and I. Also, giving honor to a mother's life, not a run through, at times it feels so out of control without dominating for attentions. But I am loving the healthy process. But I learned to welcome the dam to break. Each step a lighter footprint through the valley of the shadow. A shadow must pass to make way for the sunshine! It's really the shadow passing, and this scripture catapulted me to step into another dimension of healing through grief. I had one counseling appoint with one of the pastors at our church. He shared the same scripture with me. Within 15 minutes, I was freed to grief, Each step was a step towards hope arising. After one year on my mom's home-going anniversary, I burst out laughing. It seemed like I was the only one not planning on moaning and groaning, and it was like releasing and allowing mom to complete her cycle of life, and now the baton has been passed to me. This also prepared me for a two-year period when about eleven people passed within 2 years. 3 elders/uncles, a very dear friend, a father and mother in the faith as well as relatives and associates (Yes, I had a conversation with the father, it was quite a Dad and Daughter talk, with tears and boogers but always peace and reassurance.)

Prepped for comfort: About 12 hours before my mother's passing, I was back in the U.S for less than ten days, attending to my usual work and catching up on routines. A call from my brother around 10:00 am which was 10:00pm in Hong Kong. He reported that mom is stabled. Just after I hung up the phone. God showed me an open vision that lasted about one minute. I saw two transparent columns, milky white clouds hazy within each column. The pillars rested on each of my mom's shoulders down to her arms on both sides, with the top reaching to the ceiling of her hospital room. I looked and saw my mom looking very rested and she had a little girl's look! There must have been dozens of tiny white angelic figures energetically jumping up and down within the two cloudy columns. They seemed happily swirling on both sides of my mother. My heart knew the time must be near, and my next thought was to grab the next flight to be with her.

Minutes later, another amazing comfort came from my son's phone call. Our 7-year-old granddaughter had urgently nudged her daddy (my son) to phone grandma (me) and shared on the phone what she saw in a dream. She described her dream of standing by a stream where a tiny angel of Asian feature appeared. The angel motioned her to open one hand. When she did, the angel placed drops of water on her opened palm. She felt an urge to talk to me about her dream. I asked her about her thoughts, and she replied: Grandma, it felt so sweet and special! And she had to relate her special feeling to me.

My thoughts were, indeed, that it was sweet and special, we were both comforted and I received a preparation in advance, not an easy journey but special sweetness for my granddaughter and I, it was the most grievous year of a daughter's life. My mom passed peacefully less than 10 hours after the vision. We returned for the funeral two weeks before the riots in June of 2019. What followed was that the world began its shut down frenzy!!

Often, it's easy to be openly discuss physical symptomatic pain, but authentic emotional pain and grief demand expression before healing can come. Within a 3 years period, I had 13 people: Started with my mother, spiritual father, spiritual mother, a dear friend, uncles and aunt passed. I learn not to disallow the grief, if you are stuck, the most common action is to make demands of our current emotional reserve to meet the unpaid debts! The good grieving was that I practiced on myself to becoming a brave heart.

CHAPTER 6

HUMOR AND LAUGHTER ARE THERAPEUTICS.

◆

Isolation and loneliness are universally twin weapons leading to helplessness. These conditions rob us of strength and true joy. To become isolated is being kept apart from others which eventually may lead to lost opportunities of meaningful friendship. Loneliness is loss of connections. Often isolation and loneliness are rooted in unwarranted fear. From Dr. S.I. McMillen's book: Peace does not come in capsules, and It's not just what you eat – rather it's what eats you!

In the context of functional medicine, we consider such conditions as being lethal against whole person wellness. During a functional medicine conference I attended, one doctor emphasized that no amount of supplementation can help loneliness.

During recent years, there has been great damage to our society; rebuilding is being prepared and is required. Understanding how we contributed to alienations resulting in the damage to our society is an important question to answer. America has been a great melting pot with culturally diverse backgrounds from all nations. Ever wonder how someone living in America for 30 years and still cannot speak English fluently? I dare say "individualism" has become a form of religion. I came to America at the age of nineteen because of the gracious invitation extended to me by an American couple with three little ones. They unofficially adopted me, ensuring me a job. Within a week, I was in school and continuing my education. Heaven graced my heart to enable me to take a great big step of faith to leave all behind to go to a new country.

The culture shock and the diet changes were big adjustments for me. I was an unbelieving Christian raised up in a system of religion which was heavy in education but void of identity, faith, and love. I left it all, I became underlined available and adapting well because I wanted to, not because I had to. It's about receiving and not getting!

With the same language and no other dialects in America, there were more cynical remarks made that accompany criticizing the hearer, for not being able to take a joke. They were most hurtful for me to adapt. Like any tool, humor can be used in both positive and negative ways. I learned to shield my heart and discern the intentions of those I communicated with. Some conversations really hijacked all good intentions. You may resonate with how words can be disguised as humor which alienate connections, so much are an unhealed wound as the war is from within:

- Are you trying to share a mutual laugh to create connection?
- Is the joke at another person or group's expense?

- Do you have any hidden agenda, and you want to get an opinionated criticism in?

- Are you a mean-spirited chameleon, sending insults even when framed as a joke?

- Are you making jokes out of every situation, hiding from deeper relational intimate deficiency?

- Jealousy may loudly express biting humor or an added hostile edge to them!

I have heard the following discussions among true learners. This is quite an undeviating test because life serves back in the coin you pay. The irrevocable principle works from heaven downwards. God looks not only at the act, but He also looks at the possibility. I sincerely hope you have faith to believe this statement. The things we scrutinize/criticize in others; we are guilty of it ourselves? The reason we see hypocrisy, fraud and unreality in others is because they are all in our own hearts. The mouth reveals what's in the heart, no matter how hard they tried to disguise themselves, it shows up if there's bitterness any place inside.

Men or women, beautiful gorgeously made up too, it will explode from the inside out.

The truth is that we are created for the purpose of family and communities. Having a <u>childlike</u> attitude and demeanor are necessary qualities to show up and engage with others (notice I did not say childish). Subsequently I was introduced to laugh therapy.

"Laughter is timeless, imagination has no age, and dreams are forever."

Walt Disney

Early 2005, we relocated to a new state. As we were new to town, I showed up at a church home group. There I met a new papa in the faith: Dr. Gerald Ellison, Ph.D., (A real person deserving honorable mentioned here.) a beloved psychologist in the Mind-Body Medicine program of Cancer Treatment Centers of America in Tulsa, Oklahoma. He was a Christian Counselor, Assistant Professor of the Graduate School of Theology and Ministry at Oral Roberts University.

Dr. Ellison loved people. He taught and implemented Laugh Therapy for the oncology patients and the medical staff. He helped people to identify and mobilize their own strengths and resources towards breakthroughs. Dr. Ellison was known as the beloved psychologist and counselor to so many! However, he was so much more to me. When I arrived, my availability made possible for another divine connection. Very few people are even aware that there are fathers and mothers in the faith who are waiting for redemptive assignments.

In the New Testament Paul wrote, "I do not write this to shame you, but to warn and counsel you as my beloved children. After all, though you should have ten thousand teachers in Christ, yet you do not have many fathers in Christ", (I Cor. 4:14-15a AMP).

I am fully convinced that Father God creates and hangs the stars of the universe. In the context of the above scripture: Like many faithful servant-leaders, Dr. Ellison faithfully stewarded himself well as I postured to receive it. He skillfully "anchored God's stars," facilitated a secure hold, and a devoted safeguard for many successful leaders. He fully accessed the grace from heaven as a father seeks to distill the prophetic gifts to emerge. He also exhorted me to write and publish books, which only a good father can!

As stewardship demands accountability, I became a real daughter in the process! Humor and laughter were more facets of wholesome relational connection with this gentle giant. He often greeted everyone with this phrase: How are you percolating today? It was part of the healing arts he had cultivated.

A very special nurse friend, Tammy, remarked that "Dr. Ellison was like an angel that showed up on my worse day at work (with the sick and dying), but I was so refreshed at his laugh therapies!" My questions to you: are your tied to helplessness? Will you show up and engage a process of ultimately becoming: the best version of you?

Humor and laughter are also good exercises for the endocrine system. Laughter has been shown to have physiological, psychological, social, spiritual, and quality-of-life benefits. Adverse effects are very limited. Rarely do I hear reports of someone getting sick from laughter. There are no contraindications. Therapeutic efficacy of laughter is mainly derived from spontaneous laughter (triggered by external stimuli or positive emotions) or self-induced laughter (triggered by oneself at will).

I have worked around hospitals, clinics, physicians and dentists. My husband served as an anesthesiologist at the same hospital. He oversaw

"The Comfort Team" where having compassion is the main thing. Being patient centric, by patient's request, humor and laughter literally invade the patient's room:

Top Ten Requirements for Being a Great Doctor:

1. Endure workplace embarrassment for the sake of the patients.
2. Must be able to do the Chicken Dance.
3. Be able to assess if a patient is hallucinating or if it is your costume.
4. Represent all departments in case you can't remember where you are from.
5. Must keep up with the latest fashion, even if it requires wearing bubble wrap.
6. Keep a blow dryer on hand in case your water gun leaks in your pocket.
7. Must be ready to sing on demand.
8. Must be able to transform into a California Raisin as needed.
9. Must be able to talk to patients while chewing on silly string.
10. Must be able to "shoo" a cow!!!

Unknown to us the "Comfort Round" was so well received that God divinely infused us with the entire staff of oncologists and we brought the same concept to South China. Their hospital was so receptive that God met us with many salvations including doctors and spouses. We are born to be solutions. Several doctors' work and home relationships started a transformation process, we showed up and God did the rest. Different types of churches asked us to teach and model what we practiced at home. Laugh Therapy became a source of comfort, and we had patients waiting at the elevators asking when we will come to their floor for the "Comfort Rounds." The work continues even while we are not in the country.

From comfort to laughter, we serve the couples, doctors, co-workers, and marriage couples, it spread to an international church in Hong Kong. The establishment of these events was seamless because we made no announcements, no advertising. Literally, God was the Chef, and I was His waitress and my wonderful husband set the tables whenever he can travel to join me. The implementation required my wholehearted commitment to travel, purchasing an apartment, the furnishings, from bicycle, motorcycles, bus, trains, and flights. We just showed up. A couple of visits turned into 11 years with total abandoned love. A father's fingerprint is never far from the daughter/son: Dr. Ellison's laugh therapies apparently blazed a trail for us. He would be too humble to acknowledge but we all are recipients of GRACE: Heaven's divine influence and enablement to do Father's extraordinary transformative works as ordinary children becoming sons and daughters. Laughter and humor brought people groups together over ten counties in a city the size of Dallas, Texas. Our eyes were opened to goodness all around. A lot of memories will be packed into the next book: "*In the Moment of His Moment!" coming in 2024.*

Similar benefits may also be activated by yourself, with one or the other, in a community framework, to demonstrate that laughter is an all-around healing agent. In an era of evidence-based medicine, it is most appropriate for laughter to be used as a complementary or alternative medicine in some of the prevention and treatment of illnesses.

A sense of gentle humor can be the key to resiliency; to weather disappointments and to hold up tensions between extremes. Humor can also help to reframe a problem, such as a well-timed sense of humor easing strains and stress disarming disagreement. Truth be told, as a foreigner, I was so slow to catch some dry humors, it takes weeks later and I started to L.O.L, my husband would chime in and chuckled, "Mary finally got that joke!!!!" my timing is still off but it's improving greatly. When you laugh with one another, a positive bond is created. This bond acts as a strong buffer against stress or disappointments, in addition, laughter can be very contagious. Just hearing someone laughing will generally prime you to smile, being refreshed and you will turn to join in the fun.

Children are the real deal, the unhindered purity of being human. They own their unmatched authorities, especially as young children! When engaging with them, they know and trust you. It is the best way to get back in touch with the playful kid inside each of us. Unless we have childlike faith, we shut down ourselves as well as heaven!

Are you ready? We have two amazing grandchildren that keep me young. When they flew in to have grandparents visit, bedtime stories and humorous rituals are our kodak precious moments! There was this one time together in the same bedroom, when the younger one was barely seven, he is our little big man, he motioned me to draw near so that both his hands reached up to my face. He drew me near and cupped my face, gazing deeply into my eyes and stroking my face gently. I waited 5 seconds and I asked curiously, "what's on your mind?" as I was very curious by now. He said ever so tenderly, "I love you grandma and I wanted to tell you something special just about you, grandma!!" Now he has my full attention! He waited another second, without hesitation, he asked in the form of a question: "Grandma, do you know when you speak, you are missing not all of them, but a lot of the letter "S" in your plural(s)?"

It was the sensitivity of how he engaged me that I was lost for words. It's a beautiful interlude that was almost romantic. I stopped for a second, thoughtfully I asked how long had he noticed this? He replied: "A long time!!!" I was about to inquire if it was concerning to him. Suddenly my granddaughter bolted up and interrupted us, she spoke up with a strong passionate indignant tone to her brother: "That's my grandma, and I like her talking that way, I don't want her to change. That's what makes her different and special!" we glanced at each other for a moment and bursted out laughing and hugging as we are deepening the grannie bonding!

I once heard from a wise young teenager who leads herself well, and still resonates in my heart: "I have an <u>audience of One</u>!" She confidently trusted that God is able and hears every word she speaks!

Transparency and thoughtful courtesy are twins that are much needed today. True humility brings deference to build up, to gather and not scatter. Good humor and laughter refresh the soul of the hearer! Laughter is timeless, Imagination has no age, and Dreams are forever! This too is maximize wellness!

CHAPTER 7

NON-INVASIVE THERAPIES
AND DIVINE HEALING

———◆———

I share this topic because I am passionate about letting my readers know what's on the horizon, especially regarding preventive therapies and for recoveries. My aim is that good will and hope are all around. Let me introduce you to what I and others have benefited tremendously.

You can also find out what is of excellent quality in your area or are welcome to visit the website. I call it supporting yourself at a cellular level. The key is the effectiveness with non-invasive devices assisting the body, to activate its innate healing capacities before a serious disease shows up.

Recent global health challenges also brought out some excellent preventive therapies. Some have long been successful in Europe, and now welcomed in the US. Some of these are in medical and chiropractic facilities. They are FDA cleared or approved therapies, these are the best-known non-invasive devices I used at my previous clinical practices and have seen spectacular results. These are now available at my educational events.

Alternative Therapies in Health and Medicine:

Practice of the Future: Integrated View of Care by Christopher Bump, D.C.: Patient must remain in the center of the wheel, so that specific modalities and therapeutics offered contribute to the whole person, and patient's needs are met. 1. The practitioner must meet every patient as an individual and develop personalized interventions with them. 2. Patient must be coached that they are the hub of the wheel and that their willingness to participate in their own healing. Making lifestyle changes are paramount for success. For clinical nutrition practices, working with real people in real world situations, we are dealing with an infinite range of variability or response to change. Main themes: Health care will become patient centered: consumer. 2. Technology will become a major player to be embraced. 3. Real, whole food nutrition as foundation for real and lasting changes addressing chronic disease. 4. Emotions and Beliefs drive behavior, and behavior governs choices. Our choices manifest in healthy outcomes. www.systemsbiology.org/research/100k-wellness-project/

PEMF Exercise (FDA Cleared) Pulsed Electromagnetic Magnetic Field therapy benefits inflammation and discomfort, they are the signs of cellular imbalance.

One of my guests flew in from L.A., she could not sleep well especially from all day traveling, plus the time change and needing much rest. She was not skeptical understandably, but she was hesitant! I was so glad she accepted my suggestion. She noted that her sleep improved immediately, it showed how well the PEMF therapy worked. Additionally, she took time to email me about her follow up experience which I had no way of anticipating the quality outcome, she experienced deep tissue detox even post therapy which was impressive to me. A month later she sent me her testimony below:

Guest Testimony:

A PEMF Retreat Client's immediate experience 2022: *"I am new to PEMF therapies and received 4-(10 minutes) sessions for overall wellness initially for sleep purposes. In general, I am in very good health with current blood tests, say with confidence that blood tests showing all major markers within the normal range. That said, I was not sure what to expect from my PEMF experience –but I experienced deeper, more restful sleep from these short sessions.*

In addition, I happened to be recovering from a cold while receiving PEMF therapy. About a week after the final & fourth session, my sinuses expelled an unprecedented amount and sort of debris. Even after a functional rhinoplasty a decade ago (which helped my breathing significantly). I have never experienced airways this open and clear. To say I am thrilled with my PEMF experiences is an understatement!" Kate

PEMF exercise is a safe and effective way to support and enhance cellular energy needs and has been shown over 40 years to help with the following, and as a result, PEMF has been known for improving and supporting the following:

The Immune system.

Help to relax muscles.

Provide support for the nervous system.

Support healthy lung function.

Support healthy joint and cartilage function.

Helps reduce joint discomfort.

Helps stimulate bone growth.

"An ounce of prevention is worth a pound of cure."

Benjamin Franklin 1705 -1790

https://youtu.be/GEDoEk89NhI

Retreat Wellness Spa Testimony (2022):

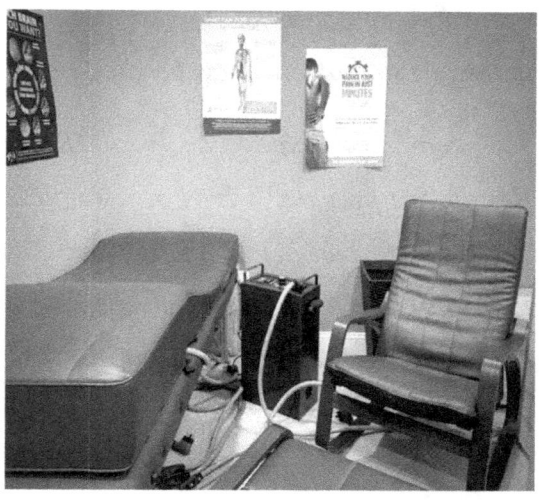

In 2022, I attended the Rekindle Retreat/Spa 4 days event at Drs. Mark & Mary Axness' facility. The timely breakthroughs and rest were deeply needed. The various therapy sessions helped me beyond my expectations.

Every meal was of culinary standard, and I was treated with skillful and thoughtful attentiveness. My experience at Rekindle Retreat/Spa reignited my passion to a new level I had not known before (over 4 years of pain and trauma). I received compassion, respect and restoration in my body, soul, and spirit. I was fully heard, coached, and counseled in an honest and safe environment.

My Rekindle Retreat/Spa experience was so positively impactful for my whole person wellness upgrade, that I engaged with Rekindle Health for further therapies over ten sessions spread over 10 weeks. Dr. Mary ran a full set of Functional lab work and evaluated me with supplements specific to my needs. The PEMF, Ozone and detoxing therapies, were most rejuvenating. I came away from each session with fresh energy and encouragement.

Several areas due to physical and emotional exhaustions. I received 30% to 75% noticeable improvements in my body. Dr. Mary's professionalism and compassionate support encouraged me to implement a new level of optimism to maximize life! My career life in the banking industry also took on a new height.

My combined experience with Rekindle Health and Rekindle Retreat/Spa provided a level of restoration in my life that exceeded my expectations. This is a wonderfully unique, once in a lifetime experience everyone deserves! There is no place I am aware of that offers such a combination of redemptive nurturing, encouraging, and envisioning me to a new capacity like Rekindle Retreat/Spa. Whb, Atlanta, GA

A fruitful analogy of cellular vitality…

Imagine a cell in your body as a fresh grape; healthy, vibrant, and alive. Now imagine that same cell as a raisin; once a vibrant

Keeping Cells 'Ripe', Not Rotting

A fruitful analogy of cellular vitality…

grape, drained and dry of all its vitality. This illustration of cellular decay is like what happens when your body lacks the energy to perform optimally.

My personal experience is that post traveling or if I have been exhausted from gardening, I would lay on the PEMF bed. After the subtle pulsing sensation for 20-30 minutes, the result is I can run up the steps vs. slow dragging motions. Frankly, it is such a phenomenal experience, my patients and now retreat attendees have been impressed. Especially for post-concussion trauma recovery. Also, one patient who is not my client, an older retired doctor. after diagnosed with early onset Alzheimer in his 70's. Whenever he feels sluggish he would get a session of 30 minutes, and he would be able to go out doing gardening and most activities. It is simple and non-invasive. A consent form is required, we recommend not wearing metals, and not if you have electronic implants like a pacemaker.

Retreat Spa Testimony 2021:

As a professional life strategist coach, and a concert pianist. I had severe low back pain while attending Dr. Axness' retreat/Spa. After one 20 minutes session, I was able to leave for the airport nearly forgetting that morning I was bending over with low back pain.

D.B. L.A.,Ca

BEMER: Another PEMF (Portable and easier for travel and very affordable)

High quality PEMF for home use especially for families, serves all the above in about 8 minutes, is subtle and my best non-invasive and preventive piece of equipment. Also, it is very quiet, and it has a sleep mode, which is perfect for laying over the mattress, and is extremely helpful with post-concussion recovery, muscular, structural and tissue regenerative support. (All PEMF equipment are contradicted for anyone who has electronic implants.)

Bemer helps reinforce all the steps that I'm taking in preventative care, so I can live a long, healthy, and active life. I started using BEMER twice a day for 8 minutes and it dramatically improved my energy levels – I feel great." Brooke Burke, TV host, fitness guru, podcaster, author, mother of four and philanthropist.

The uniqueness of Bemer lies in its signal and its configuration. The signal leads to scientifically grounded stimulation of the smallest vessels (microcirculation) supporting the circulator system. No other biophysical modality in the world targets the microcirculation in the way

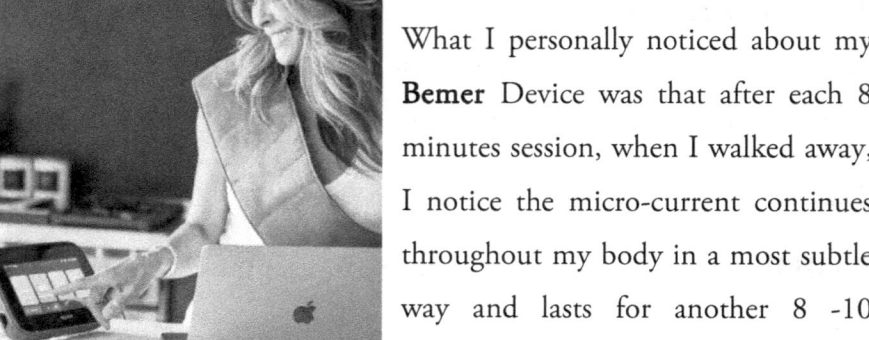

that Bemer does.

What I personally noticed about my **Bemer** Device was that after each 8 minutes session, when I walked away, I notice the micro-current continues throughout my body in a most subtle way and lasts for another 8 -10 minutes, especially if I keep in my rest mode. It works from the inside out. I am quite experienced in these forms of therapies to share with everyone, you cannot go wrong with getting a **Bemer** (be very aware of knock offs, do not be confused with a mail ordered tens unit. It may sound so similar, but not durable and without the true therapeutic effects and supports I come to expect). I like it so much; I acquired the training supported by becoming a qualified distributor.

<u>Ozone:</u> Especially good for any compromised immune system, your cells might be lacking in their ability to produce adequate healthy cell wall protection. enzymes, catalase, superoxide dismutase (SOD), and glutathione peroxidase (GPx), these enzymes work in tandem to help prevent damage to healthy cells from free radicals, they protect cell walls by forming a barrier as the immune system uses Reactive Oxidant Species (commonly known as a free radicals), ROS accomplish this by penetrating the microbes' cell walls, spilling out the debris contents, another form of detoxing, effectively destroying the microbe or infection.

<u>Another story as an illustration</u>: A lady who had just been through life's major events including the death of a spouse and her son's suicide, all within 2.5 years' time. She was a clogdancer and a sweetheart of a piano teacher at the public school, multi-talented musician of every musical instrument, she just has the most upbeat personality and beautifully resilient attitude about life and was most cheerful. However, as I observed her tolerance and rationalizing her condition. she has no knowledge of what I do and can offer her. Not being pushy at all. But this time, I knew I could do something for her spiraling downward condition.

The emotional traumas had exasperated her chronic inflammations. As a diabetic, she also sustained an unhealed nail wound on one foot from dancing. When she came, she was unable to walk with severe edema and unable to keep her shoe on one foot. She had lost sensations on both legs from the knee down. She was on the pic-line, and her doctor informed her she may eventually need amputation of one foot.

When she came in for an initial consultation, I prescribed supplements and placed her on a bed, and I applied ozone throughout her body. I seriously prayed and tried to do what I know with complimentary medicine, with her physician's approval! After every session of about 30 minutes each visit, a total of 5 sessions), she would feel so good that she needed no help to walk up the 200-foot sloped driveway to the parking lot. She was so excited that she could feel the breeze against her legs. To my knowledge, she is very efficient in her wheelchair keeping both legs and feet, last I heard about 3 years ago, she was living a full life, giving piano lessons, holding recitals for her students in her own house, and maintaining over one acre of outdoor gardening. I applaud her zest for life, and she inspired me to give my best.

As a practitioner, I worked alongside without being antagonistic towards western physicians. We need both at times. I do not condone the recent pharmaceutical hog washing. But I continue to be amazed with 100% of the beautiful people sent to me by word of mouth. I put my supportive hat on, listened and always start with understanding the cause, next with nutrition counseling and supplement to bring some needed nutrient fast, everyone returned with firsthand improvement. An exit interview is need so both sides recognized either intermittence usage of therapies is needed before signed off with 50%-100% satisfactory. Then they would go tell someone. Servanthood with compassion is always the best form of doctoring. The truth is that the more I know, the more I can learn.

<u>Sauna</u>: Steam and Dry: a bather's circulation.

Cutaneous circulation increases greatly in sauna to prevent body heating. The effects of both heat and cold are mediated via the sympathetic nervous system. The circulatory responses to sauna are related to the intensity and duration of the heat exposure. An ordinary sauna bath increases cardiac workload about as much as moderate or vigorous walking.

Also, sauna is a therapeutic tool, in addition to components of practical clinical detox programs it is highly effective for certain cardiovascular problems. It enhances the mobilization of fat-soluble xenobiotics, to help reduce blood pressure and enhance blood flow, micro-circulation is most beneficial. You will be hearing more about it now; it is extremely popular in Japan and many eastern and European nations. Sauna is considered a detox measure to enhance the mobilization of heavy metals and chemical xenobiotics. Saunas are safe and effective for relaxation purposes, being that 15 minutes per session is most adequate. Always let someone know if you are taking a sauna bath alone or exceeding 15 minutes. There is too much other evidence supporting benefits indirectly.

Altern Ther Health Med.,2007 Mar-Apr; 13(2): S154-6

I find every form of sauna therapy to be a special time to relax, to clear the noise, declutter the mind and rest. Most people enjoy a short evening session for the good night's sleep they get. In addition, if you travel especially to Japan, South Korea, (in selective European countries as well). Hot springs with varieties of mineral springs are most popular, it's very therapeutic to relax and allow yourself to soak and unwind, always you will find male and females in separate quarters. In northern Asian it's a regular practice for elderlies, you will find more women using steam sauna and various baths for circulation purposes. You will find that more than 50% are older folks, honestly, no one cares to stare at your bodies, they are more health conscious than body conscious. In the US especially in large metropolitan cities, you can inquire of spa like Korean bath houses, they are equipped with mineral salt rooms, herbal baths, hot and cold pools for exfoliation, rest and rejuvenation to optimize wellness. Afterall, most mothers are working 24-7. There are some that are equipped with even juice bar and snacks available after your baths therapies.

Cold Laser Therapy:

Laser therapy has been successfully used globally for over 30 years, LLLT Low Level Laser is painless, sterile, non-invasive, drug-free application, which is used to treat a variety pain syndromes, injuries, wound, fracture, neurological conditions, and pathologies. When acceleration of healing from injuries is desired, it is safe, proven, sessions are more affordable and well documented since 1985. It has become a medical therapy for healing wounds and fractures up to 60% faster. In the U.K., LLLT has become the treatment of choice for soft tissue injuries. Cautions if you are seeking laser equipment, make sure you can return and get a full refund if you are not happy. I am extremely careful with any laser equipment since I am acquainted with too many, and I usually took time to learn about the manufacturer, the efficacy of the designs. When it comes to quality preventive healing therapy equipment, I am among the first to be given introductions. Therefore, I am selective what I use. Most importantly, I waited and then I ran it through my physicians for their opinions. Finally, I tried it on myself and family members. In my 20+ years of wound healing, detox had been an asset to my personal and professional experiences.

I have had a history of low back sciatica pain for over 30 years. Certain exercise and stretching helped but it flared up whenever stress or emotional events triggered pain. At times, the pain was so intense that I had ringing in my ears, and much lost sleep as well. Dr. Larry Altshuler, M.D., who was a beloved physician at the Cancer Treatment Center, Tulsa, OK (he has since passed in 2021)

Dr. Altshuler treated my back twice within a week. While my back was not completely cured, the treatment I received kept me pain free for about 10 years. I was so impressed that I asked my doctor a lot of questions regarding the Cold Laser Therapy.

Dr. Altshuler introduced me to the original owner manufacturer, and we met and they trained me for clinical applications. As the owner of this 830nm non thermal FDA approved device, I travel with mine.

Results are:

- Increased collagen production
- Enhanced nerve regeneration

- Increased vasodilation

- Reduced inflammatory duration

- Increased cell metabolism

- Increased pain threshold

- Reduced edema magnitude

- Increased microcirculation

- Increased tissue and bone repairs

- Increased lymphatic response.

This type of laser is quite passive, having no shocks or pulsating as with electronic stimulation nor heat used with ultrasounds. The only sensation is the touch of the probe head as it meets the skin surface. The number of sessions and duration depends upon the severity of the condition. Generally, immediate change is observed at the first session. Usually, 4-5 sessions are effective or 8-12 in chronic to severe conditions.

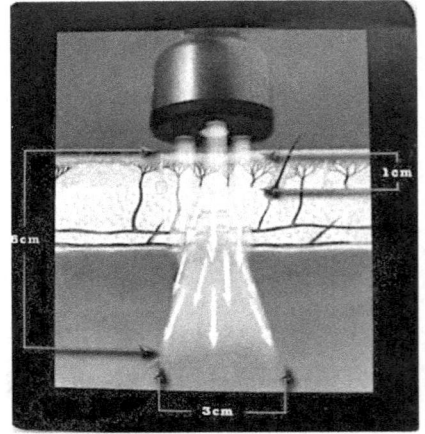

No known contraindications: if there are known cancer, pregnancy, Not for the Eye areas and only lower facial areas (Consents Forms are required).

Pictures of Acute Wound Healing: right hand (share with permission on file) Q.G., GA

Below are before and after pictures I treated in 2022. This was my retreat guest. He and his wife were attendees and had experienced all our noninvasive wellness therapies.

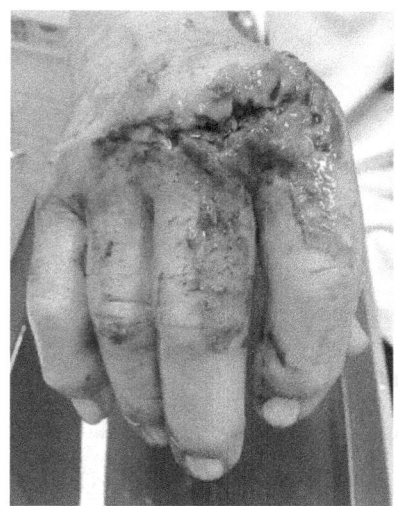 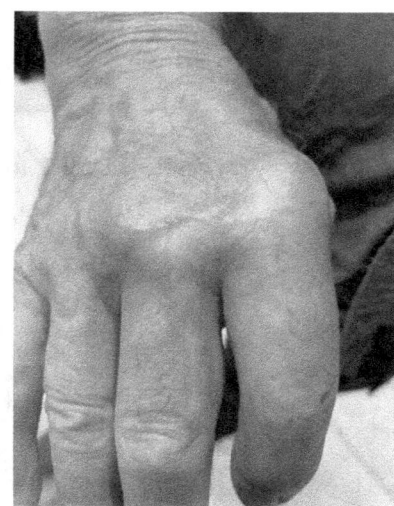

Before and after pictures I helped in 2022 (A severe bike accident.)

A few months after the retreat, I learned that they just recovered from COVID. He got into a serious bicycle accident. I sent them to the Grady Trauma One center twice in Atlanta to seek a hand surgeon. They had some experienced the effectiveness of all the equipment at my facility from a retreat setting, they sent me the picture on the left side above. Clinically I was concern and not qualify without my M.D.'s approval, therapeutically I had no doubt I could help. He had to follow up with his part to consult a hand surgeon. Without putting anyone in a bad light, twice he returned asking for help with what I have available. With medical oversight, I was not skeptical at all, however the severed nerve only God can supervised, not to mention the high possibility of infection it was about 5-6 days of the trauma. Also, it's his dominant hand, which will require trauma care and a hand specialist. He agreed and signed a consent for me to help him along with necessary supplements.

I supported him for the extreme pain along with what was dispensed from his hometown urgent care, getting adequate sleep. As well as a host of supplements for tissue regeneration, laser and other self-regenerative therapies. After a total of 7 sessions within 5 weeks duration…even though his index finger only regained partial but not full range of motions. All indication was he kept his hand and elbow, entire arm intact. And he was so please and less than months later, he was able to do gardening! When so much quality auxiliary care was unavailable during COVID. I was thankful that this gentleman was well served in this unusual setting. I continue to encourage him to pursue a hand surgeon for tendon reconnection.

Following are my three Healing Testimonies:

An Enlarged Lymph pronounced with days to live:

July 18-21, 1999, I received supernatural healing when the physicians gave me 3-4 days to live. God's total mercy and healing power override all and Jesus guided me with His Word literally came alive to receive grace and strength, and brought boldness for me to pray in the Holy Spirit, in tongue for 2 nights and 3 days nonstop light and life filled my body. I left the hospital with no medication, no surgeries. See details on

Part II Chapter. 4 "Drips of Resentment"! God is my Healer. A few years later, When I was willing to inquire and became receptive to learn my lesson: I was playing with deadly emotions of unforgiveness, I allowed anger and its trauma effects to invade my body. Thus, the reason that I keep His testimony alive. Let this be my loud voice returning to glorifying our first Healer, In Luke 17:14-18 Christ Jesus said, there were ten got healed, and I am amazed that one foreigner who keep returning to thank Lord Jesus by His Spirit, I received. My healing and Luke 17:20-21 The kingdom of God is within us!

(Disclaimer: I do advocate that a believer need the Body of Christ, the church will continues its appointed functions, for the 5-fold ministers must arise. See Ephesians Chapter 4: 9-13 to be equipped and all come to the unity of the Faith)

Head Concussion: Florida department store:

October 14, 20014, We were in Florida for the birth of our grandson, as soon as our son's family was fine for me to show up, I drove there fully with a mother's heart to do whatever to help our daughter-in-love's recovery (a touch of "month sitting" from Asian post-partum care), and my husband flew in, to welcome our grandson.

By the 7th day, I was tired and needed some personal time, laying down I realized I could acquire a few items to replenish her kitchen (which she was so graciously receiving!), Also, I could use a pair of sandals. A Shoe rack which I held onto kept me from a worse un-imaginable nightmare… A piece of flying luggage came from one or two isle back flew over and knocked me on my head, the injury hit me at such force resulted in a concussion. I lost balance with a loud scream, and I was disoriented. Until I saw a piece of luggage flew from behind over the isle(s), hit me on the heard and landed on the floor 3' by my feet. Hindsight, I should have called an ambulance. The store manager brough ice and felt the swelling, meanwhile I was seeing stars. Subsequently, the following 2 years, daily I struggled with severe headaches, insomnia, loss of frontal memory and speech functions. Classroom seminars were like watching the speaker's mouth moves with slow response time and was only 20-25% of my normal comprehension, up/down stairway movements required very careful coordination. I had a most un-sympathetic neurologist whose only suggestion was a script for anti-depressive meds just to support sleep. There were no meds for the brain! Also, after all being over 65, I was lectured not to be too ambitious!

But I have strong faith and a big heart, therefore, I began to imagine the future assignment of my house to become a healing retreat center with the Word of God under the tiles and carpeted floors. And God honored my desire to fulfill the calling. Meanwhile, at Bethel I used my convalescent time to attend BASSM, Bethel Atlanta School of Supernatural Ministry. During which a most credible apostolic (5-fold) minister came to speak. I purchased his book at the author's table, who taught about the gift of forgiveness; Michael Maiden from Arizona, he passed me on his way leaving after his teaching, seeing me he stopped and asked my name, sat me down and declared: God has a hose over your head to filling you up like a reservoir" and there are people you need to forgive, 2 woman and some men. (I knew instantly who they were, I prayed for my enemies and release them to Christ Jesus! It's part of a recovery step.)

Within two weeks at my dining table, where I sat after prayer time. I sensed a pair of firm hands cupping and massaging my heard, it heated up like hot oil all over my brain penetrating like it's on fire. And I knew God is healing and restoring my brain, when I got up from my dining chair, I looked at the clock, the heavenly massage went on for over 45 minutes! The blessings are beyond anything tangible for this lifetime to behold.

2016 on my daughter's birthday, the Lord gifted me this Abiding Word: At each sunrise we will be thanking you for your kindness and your love. As the sun sets and all through the night, I will keep proclaiming, "You are so faithful!" Psalm 92:2 (TPT)

Pour the oil of your Spirit upon my soul. As I place all my affection upon you, I will thrive in your heavenly courtyard. Teach me to abide faithfully in this place of full surrender, so that even in my old age, I will be strong and fresh, bearing fruit for all to savor.

By Brian Simmons (Prayers on Fire, 365 days praying the Psalms)

A car accident at night:

February 19, 2019. Driving my brand-new Tahoe, ever so cautious on this misty wet cold Tuesday night around 9 pm from ministry school. Just coming out after a full stop at a quiet intersection. A speeding car came at me at such force that it hit my car twice on the left side. I became unconscious after I saw a flashing light and only remembered a loud noise, "BOOM" I avoided the mental trauma, God wired the body to shut down, this is a way to protect from the shock, I learned from school. A sweet friend driving on the same road in passing saw the horrific scene, she climbed inside the driver side wishing to help and offer prayer, another fellow Lee, remained in another car on the same road simply stayed in his car and prayed (not knowing it was Mary Axness). I still didn't know who called my husband or the ambulance. When I awaken and said, "Tabatha, why are you inside my car?" With a reassuring voice, she told me I was seriously hurt, the ambulance is on the way. She contacted my husband and the Bethel leader, Dan Weber, who notified others for prayers. The ambulance arrived, and the paramedic was reassuring me that I was seriously injured, and he notified the Grady Trauma One Center in Atlanta. Meanwhile, I noticed I was unable to move from my chin down, and my husband came, I recognized him, but I was able to give him some eye contact. Then we were on our way toward midtown. Again, I had no fear whatso ever, and trusted the Spirit of Jesus is the resurrection power activating in me, He can raise me up, He's able and is working on me now, the whole way, I hummed, but I realized the paramedic was connecting with the Trauma Center, directing him as he was busy taken care of many preliminaries, he has a sweet spirit, and I didn't stress at all, before the ER arrival. (The whole time, Lee Frances, one of Bethel's student-ministers, he followed the ambulance all the way to the ER, he chatted with the paramedics, saw Mark's arrival before he took off, thank you, Lee and Tabatha) The whole time, I was humming the worship song: "I raised a Hallelujah!" meditating the lyrics, my melody was my weapon... For the following 48 hours stay, I was losing fluids from both ends, I could tell the medical team was very concerned, the nurses wanted to cut up my t-shirt, because I could not move, my right arm was good though, but I beg her not to cut the shirt, she was fine with it. I had a bedpan and every movement felt like the building was going to crumble, they ran too many tests, all night and I was alert filling my time with humming and singing, I could tell my Mark was scared, and was trying to hide what seems obvious from his prospective. The amazing experience was so surreal, the excruciating pain and unable to move, but distinctively very cognitive of my heart and my mind was unusually united as if my body was on the gurney and all sensory are focus on the lyrics and the melody, not easy to explain on paper. There was no bed for new admission, so I was placed in the hallway, later to the visitor's lounge where lights were on 24-7 and TV was blaring sharing the lounge with 3 other very friendly but loud patients, what I heard was the women were each having visitors. Their lunch arrived but none for me. Lo and behold, a merciful one hollered loud for the nurse on my behalf to fetch my lunch, which I didn't care for. Suddenly this sweet Asian nurse came in and ask where I was from, within minutes, we were speaking my native dialect in Cantonese, and the bonus was, she asks what I like to eat. She returned later with the biggest bowl of fresh fruit, and later she informed me that it was from another nurse' lunch, that other nurse came by my bed too, and both were so extra kind. They checked and advised me to make some movements. Now, the other women now were almost in an uproar because I got the fresh fruit. Both nurses then helped me to remove the bedpan and assisted me to get up to use the rest room. It was like I got two angels! Just by attempting, I realized I can move, and the pain was all on the left chest. It seemed like less than 8 hours later; I was ready for discharge. The humming and singing brought faith to pull kingdom come.

I had seven fractured ribs and several minor injuries, but God healed in unusual ways. John 5:17 Jesus said, My Father is working…YES, Dad, you are working on my created parts, please do what You do best, I'll received! His Rest in Hebrew 4 was very real. When I postured to receive my healings, and my inheritance, my friends, this is not religion nor theology, Father's benefits. 6 weeks later, I return for the follow up visit. The X-ray tech was so happy and surprised, remarked of the great progress. She advised that if anything unusual, I will be contacted, and I shared my experience with her, she said several amens.

Within 2 months with continued pain meds from the attending physician, I was healed completely, and no more pain, I was assured raising a Hallelujah is the melody for keeping my healing miracles.

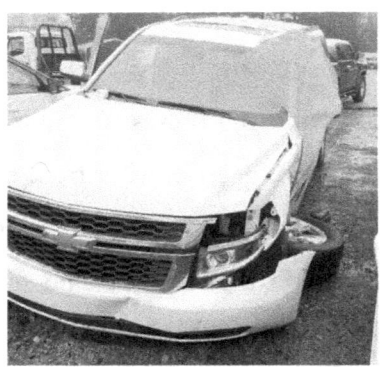 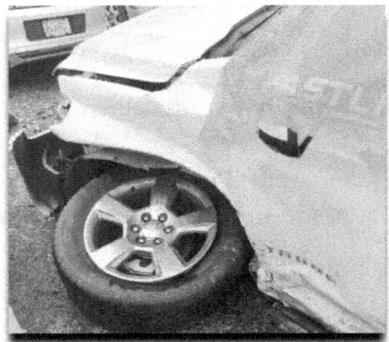

PART II
MAXIMIZE LIFE
INTRODUCTION TO FORGIVENESS

INTRODUCTION TO MAXIMIZE LIFE (PART II)
CULTIVATE FORGIVENESS

———————◆———————

Forgiveness is a gift, a lifestyle, an understanding, and a growing self-awareness of what I choose to keep within my heart and mind. I didn't realize this gift was readily available until I learned to receive and embrace it, implementation is very costly in your super-ego, nor will it be a casual thing to handle.

Forgiveness is a mental attitude to embrace, and a virtue to practice, it is the very basic inheritance gift I get to maneuver from within, thus I call it "My Father's Daughter – Embrace The Gift of Forgiveness". You never know how or when you will get to practice using this gift, it will richly reward you, and it may even preserve your life!

Apply and embrace this gift with your most genuine and generous self. Being intentional to implement, you will be paying yourself forward for many blessings yet to come, especially to stay well physically and mentally. Certainly, it will always be optional if you harness this gift delicately throughout your lifetime, this lifetime offer me unlimited access to forgive 7x70 times (Matthew 18:21 TPT).

I invite you to embark on this journey of learning or re-learning to forgive, no one can ever be so good at this or better yet, than the Master who lived and commanded this!

Note to the Reader: I do not claim to have any more knowledge about Forgiveness, Offenses and Reconciliations. I merely share with you, my readers, about what I observed and experienced. What I do know is God sees, and He is the ultimate Healer.

I continue to keep my motto: God is the Chef; I am His Waitress!!!

CHAPTER 1

OFFENSES AND RECONCILIATIONS

———————◆———————

The Sources of Offense, afflictions, and injuries against your soul! I am used to asking many what, why and how, below is a short list:

- Generational Curses
- War Crimes
- Institutions and Systems
- Religious Church Hurts
- Anger warranted and perceived.
- Toxic authorities
- Abandonment and Rejections
- Immature Authorities or Parents
- Incest
- Orphan Heart
- Sexual and Emotional Abuses
- Self-inflicted Anxious Thoughts

- Covenant – Ungodly Soul-Ties
- Peer Pressures - Intimidations
- Differing or misunderstood personalities
- False responsibilities that seemed real
- Bullies or ill-willed people
- Toxic effects of Medical Issues
- Misogyny
- Neglects or Indifferences
- Families: Siblings
- Distorted Painful Childhood.
- Distorted paradigms.
- Deceptive Self-Help Teachings

Etc., etc. The list will keep adding, allow yourself to prioritize one item to focus on. I am sure you can add more to your list. It is perfectly fine to admit being wrong, Ask the Father to show you, He does in ever such gentle ways, seek wisdom to shore up your heart, you never know how awesome you are until you walk the walk,

Every day, you can advance to discern and get wisdom towards setting proper boundaries. When and what to engage or dis-engage, while trusting God and being sure to ask for His leading. His ways and means are higher, and He leads His children with eternal purposes with your best interest, He's bigger and more caring than your problems, so glad He is God, and you are not, but you bear His image and likeness. God has capacity and destiny waiting for you!

By now, perhaps you can list your own one item or choose from the above, where is this coming from? Ask, Seek and Knock: Wait for His answers, do not lean only on your own understanding. Journaling is a most healing practice. Becoming whole requires courage, time, and investment into yourself because you are worth Him dying so you can live. Become a wholehearted healed person and behold the freedom to live well and love deeply.

Be certain to ask honestly what part did you play in contributing to the dilemma? Having been in many inner-healings trainings, I see God's beloved often has been misunderstood or unheard, and their voice and reasonings may have barricaded their growth. Rest assured God Himself holds the keys to vengeance. He will repay!

> If we get bitter toward those who offend us, we will damage our health and our enemies will control our thoughts and emotions. If we do good to them, we free God to bless us. *"Vengeance is mine; I will repay says the Lord . . . overcome evil with good"* (Romans 12:19 NKJV).

Forgiveness is not Reconciliation: Two completely different issues, forgiveness requires one party, and Reconciliation requires at least two or more parties. Not to rationalize or justify continuous inappropriate behaviors. Forgiveness focuses on the <u>offense</u>, staying true and honestly admitting that an offense or harm done, and requiring no continuing of relationship. But reconciliation focuses on <u>the relationship</u> of both parties. Reconciliation is conditional and is based on both parties' goodwill towards each other.

"Let the wise listen and add to their learning,
and let the discerning get guidance" (Proverbs 1:5)

"The wise also will hear and increase in learning, and the person of understanding will acquire skill and attain to sound counsel, (so that he may be able to steer his course rightly) (Proverbs 9:8) AMP

What Forgiveness is not: There are overwhelming misconceptions and wrong teachings, or little teaching regarding Forgiveness is a whole different matter:

Forgiveness is not excusing unjust behaviors against us.

Forgiveness is not explaining away the hurt inflicted to you.

Forgiveness is not stuffing your anger.

Forgiveness is not a conditional matter.

Forgiveness is not forgetting.

Forgiveness is not denial of hurt feelings.

Forgiveness is not circumventing God's justice.

Forgiveness is not just waiting for time to pass, time doesn't heal.

Forgiveness is not being a doormat or acting as a martyr.

An unforgiving heart can show up in various ways: Condemning, merciless, contempt, envy, maligning with intent to hurt, argumentative and critical, impatient, and easily provoked, prideful, elevating self and view others less deserving. Being unforgiven allows a bitter root to grow, opening a door to host Satan to your destruction, it will require someone to pay a betrayal. It will justify punishment and will keep the victim emotionally tied with the offender, blaming tactics as though someone must pay for the offense, he/she will unknowingly take on an interval image and likeness of their offender.

It took my mother a long time to forgive the war atrocities she witnessed as a young maiden. She had to be sent off at age 13 and was raised in other countries by two old maid aunts, she spoke three languages and two Chinese dialects. I had the privilege to help her walk through the initial unforgiveness of some major root issues. and get healed, (she had a season of seeking out godless teachings and had some mixtures of the world religion. She admitted she felt separated from God, many are not discipled.) My mom literally found it difficult to forgive the fact that she had to be separated from her seven other siblings due to national famine. When she returned to China, she had a difficult time adjusting to being the daughter she once was. The post war famine was just no less horrific than the war itself. Fortunately, she had exceptionally loving parents, and was most teachable. (She was available, willing and has simplistic faith.) As her daughter, I became a type of mentor and spiritual mother to her, only God's mercy and grace can heal half the family line. Ultimately, she led the way for both of us to minister to her own family. It was indeed amazing grace.

"In times of war, the enemy of God had gained some territory, taken grounds even generational foothold, your foe then has a secure base to further unresolved anger. I find this to be so true for the war time comfort women, especially in Southeast Asia. Lots of shame and very burdened souls were left feeling insignificant and powerless. Sometimes, holding onto wrong, fans the flames of the sense of entitlement, false power, and superiority since no one likes to feel powerless. Unforgiveness gives an illusion of power and a sense of control. By holding on to hatred, you feel infused with strength, retaliating with revenge will carry out a power play."

By Hunt, June, (2011) *How to deal with difficult relationships, Bridging the gaps That Separate People* Hope for the Heart, Inc., Harvest House Publishers

"Whoever conceals their sins does not prosper, but the one who confesses and renounces them finds mercy" (Proverbs 28:13)

CHAPTER 2

PREPARATION OF THE HEART
– MY FATHER'S DAUGHTER

A Child Learned Forgiveness: Preparation of the heart

What's not possible with men is possible with God.
(Imagination? Or an encounter with The Father?)

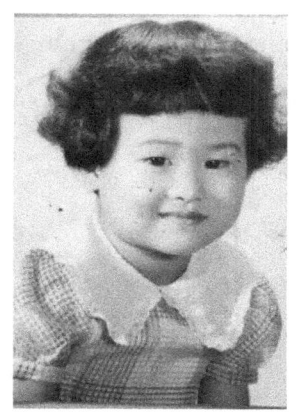

My father, the tower of a man I adored and admired. My whole little soul was to please him! Many little girls love to sit on daddy's lap for hugs and for approvals and nods of eye contact connections. Dad commanded his presence authoritatively. Generally, I recalled that before entering a room the clearing of his throat signified his presence is near. His voice was that as a "Tai-Pan" (a boss or one who led as an employer). He was a building contractor, leading a team of workers, masons, architects, accountants, contractors and laborers accounting for a 30 people crew. He was a builder with his own company, known for building condominiums for the upper middle class.

Although my father in his daily usual business attire, a 3-piece suit, he wasn't outwardly expressive with physical affections, but he has a unique way of letting me know that I am my father's daughter. Around the age of 6-7, there was a significant confirmation that I often reference until this day. It marked me for life.

My overall memories often consisted of how I promised to do all my chores for my dad by shining his shoes, having his morning newspaper ready, or simply being quiet and compliant while my mom was busy attending to my newborn sister. I kept asking my mom that I wanted some pets, asking for bunnies, and perhaps even some baby chicks as well! Mother only replied that I must keep on asking my dad for my wishes!

Seeming like a long wait, watched him built the wired structure gave me the most wonderful memory of my dad. I felt a sense of personal responsibility to take great care of my anticipated pets. Since my little sister was 4 years younger, more often than not, like most first born, I had the distinct feeling my parents set up the rabbit cage just for me. I felt like an only child. Eventually I also carried a false sense of responsibility that I needed to contribute to my parents' marital happiness!

Back then, I often whispered to my little sister that I wished she grew up faster so we could play! However, we were further divided because she has her own nanny and I have mine. On a social scale,  we had a perceived wealthy status with chauffeurs and chefs. I was somewhat sheltered, and I only interacted with few children my age. I often thought that I was my dad's one and only child, being his favorite. I idolized him!

As time went on, a couple of bunnies quickly turned into a cage full of busy mating rabbits, I recalled their bright pink eyes staring directly at me hungry for more carrots and Bok-choi (an Asian vegetable). Their beautiful fur fascinated me as to how they keep themselves ever so clean and white! I often had many questions, and I would seek answers from my dad even when he's busy. He often provided me with simple but commanding answers!

Most days my mother is very well dressed ever ready to accompany my dad for social functions. Often, she would be busy visiting friends and relatives. What appeared to me then was the women talking, talking and more talks with so much noise, but little meaning registering with me. And why were women congregating in the powder room?! My parents married by parental arranged match making. They only dated a couple of times with the family elders' approval, all based on dowry and shallow yet cordially superficial exchanges of gifts. The families would be so busy with the wedding and banquet planning. They forgo dating and relationship building, because they were consistently being watched, small band of annoyingly excited relatives often hang around. The family temple priest and elders decided the lucky day for the wedding. The venue for the big banquet (paid for by the groom's family) also dictated availability. 3-9 months are all it took for the elaborate banquet rituals, and it was all about community celebration.

And then they were married! It was merely an arrangement for my parents!!! (I must insert here; many nations' traditional parents' arranged marriages were well supported before and after the weddings. Many couples flourished well and finished stronger than they first started!)

The Taipans were very shrewd businessmen. Many of my dad's associates who were mostly "want to be" dignitaries. They borrowed from buddies until they were in positions of authority. Then most will deny ever knowing you! So many business banquets or dinner parties, countless times I heard stories of my dad's teen years involving events of how he was severely beaten by the Japanese army when they invaded Hong Kong!! (My dad had several very visible machete scares to show for, his dad lost his life during the war.) Eventually the heartbreaking announcement of my dad's bankruptcy related to giving away his company to the society larcenists. My dad was almost in jail for a debt he didn't owe. <u>He didn't listen to the wisdom of his wife.</u> Pride destroyed everything he esteemed. And that was the start of my dad's personality changes which gave way to family chaos! Along came the concubines which my father frequented. One tried to entice me to call her mommy... I politely declined but I mentally assigned her as an intruder! Thankfully I alerted my mom regarding their plot to frame my dad. The practice of polygamy was a status symbol for men then. And it was a silent crime against family and children, not to mention the devastated dishonor and devaluation of women and daughters, young and old. The Pearl of The Orient, Hong Kong, had trained me to be more street smart than I care for! Truth be told, many men betrayed themselves and violated their own families.

I witnessed the frightening verbal arguments between my parents, as dad became and more violent. Often, I would cup my little sister's ears and hover over her with my body just to protect her from occasional flying objects. I hugged her and tried to keep her crying decibel level to minimal was the best I could do! So predictable that I would find my mother crying and screaming as dad ran out of the house, gone for one or many nights. Such was the common scenery I endured as a little girl! It did, however, give me time and peace to strategize how to console a sobbing mom, picking up the broken plates dutifully. These events increased more in frequency (every few weeks) as our family grew, later adding 2 more siblings!

A similar tortuous experience while less threatening was the boring chore of being a little helper to my grandmother (dad's side). This required escorting and carrying her temple ritual necessities to the near and far Buddhist temples, as well as witnessing her praying to some monstrous looking statues. There were other sleeping statues layered with gold in the midst of smoke filled dark and musty temple rooms. Grandma would be interacting with monastery monks, just waiting around for what seemed hours. The burning incense was unbearable and nauseating! Along with the arduous moldy smelly temple visits, there were the various rituals included fortune telling. Paying money to the monks got my grandma the bamboo container half filled with pre-designated fortune sticks. These were all handwritten by someone given to those desperate souls sincerely wishing for a change of luck. Watching her whining and venting her discontentment all the way to the temple and back, we would stop en route, purchasing gold foiled origami paper. I helped her fold them and then burn them away in huge public urns. She would then bang her forehead, bowing low to the ground to secure some omen from various monks. All this did not compute in my head no less my heart. It was beyond insanity, and it had little to do with honoring ancestors represented by dead painted wooden objects. The incense burning was suffocating! Asking questions will get a one word reply, it's out customs! I had no voice in my dreaded obedience to the monthly ritual, so I stopped talking most of the time. During this period, I would talk just to myself (so I thought), asking lots of questions with no answers. There were many what's, whys and intermittent cries yearning for change.

On this one very average but beautifully sunny day, I only attended half day of kindergarten. After lunch I had an enjoyable time feeding and talking to the bunnies! I was hanging out by myself at the courtyard looking up, watching beautiful white fluffy clouds moving slowly, dressing up the clear blue sky. I was my usual daydreaming self, aimlessly still remembering how I wish I could share my special moment with just anyone! Since there weren't many neighborhood kids around, I mainly entertained myself by caring for my rabbits. And later the overpopulated 3x4 type wired cage did turn into a hen house where I was able to daily gather fresh eggs, which I took to the chef, he was a jolly guy soon got hired away, all the servants were kind and wonderful because my mom loved them. Some stayed and worked without pay for more than a year…, I believed there was where I learned to love without social class structure. All the servants stood with the family when the bottom fell out. Between bunnies, chickens eggs were my most cherished childhood moments!

What came next was a most monumental event of my life. Much later I realized that this unforgettable event was a stabilizing factor cemented into my childhood memory. <u>I may be lonely, but I am never alone.</u> Resiliency is about to take hold of my life!

Suddenly I heard a very tender but a deep voice calling my name. Looking around I saw not a soul, but myself in the outer courtyard of our big house. Although I didn't see anyone, I identified that it was a man's voice that resembled my dad's former handsome voice. I recalled asking who was there. I became very still again as I examined my surroundings. Then I heard a second time, the same voice right over my head, someone was calling for me!!! I instinctively looked up and it was as though now the sky and clouds all stood at attention. I felt very important, a sense of significance. I felt I am known by a universe with a most attentive presence. It was a lingering moment of being very special at this most impressionable age! At that moment I knew, without a shadow of a doubt, that I am known by someone so big, so high, so deep who is watching over me. Though I can't reach for this person, He was this tender being that was orchestrating the sky, the clouds and a sweet stillness all folding me into a time capsule. That precious moment, a rare delight established deep inside of me, I was captivated!

Again, I am wanted, and I am known by a strength and a wonder no one can disturbed. As a result, my own dad's countless bad behaviors and presence had become less powerful. I prayed to heaven for my dad's wellness. But watching how violent and cruel he had become, and how hopelessly mean hearted he was to his very own family. I viewed him as the tormented one! I ached with sympathy yet ashamed of him as I learned to keep my distance.

Then within months I suddenly asked my achy heart what I should do with this distanced man? A light bulb as a revelation came on! In a split second, I sensed a familiar tenderness and watchful impression spoke as I echoed out loud this reasoning: That man is no longer my dad. He is not even close to what I have known of him. Something else has "taken over my dad". He's over there (even while in the same space), and I am over here! There is an invisible divide that appeared between us. So, I asked again what I should do with this man. I heard my heart spoke: _Well, I will just have to forgive him…and I no longer allow him to occupy my heart!_

Instantly, I sensed a "letting go" from the tied down heaviness. I also sensed inside that I had moved beyond my pain and had grown up a big notch!!! At 7 years old, I had taken on a mental capacity that was way beyond my age. This new attitude that seemingly came from nowhere shaped my attitude to carry compassion, along the way equipping me to establish boundaries as a little girl!

> **Thanks to those who hurt me,** you made me a stronger person. Thanks to those who loved me, you made my heart bigger. Thanks to those who cared, you made me feel important. Thanks to those who showed concern, you let me know that you care. Thanks to those who left, you showed me that not everything is forever. Thanks to those who stayed, you showed me the true meaning of friendship. Thanks to those who entered my life, you helped me become the person I am TODAY.
> — Unknown

Today I am my FATHER's Daughter. I know well Who I belong to and Whose I am. I commit my wholehearted adoration to God, my Father, as HE will always be the One, I can lean into, my Forever Awesome Wonder. The One who called me by my name as I yearn to relate to my dad until around 7 years old. And this was and continues to be **my story**!

Looking back now, I believe that moment marked a "Big Yes" inside of me. That eventful experience prepared a reality for me to become receptive to hear the voice of my God. But it wasn't until 25 years later that I recognized that God was seeking an intimate relationship with me.

As a child, I had no way to connect, no context to build on intimacy. However, one momentary encounter forever filled much of the void in my empty soul. The Spirit of God bridged a path to a subsequent Father-Daughter encounter! In the moment of His providential moment, my Father beheld great pleasure and tirelessly worked all things together for my good! God is wholly devoted to His redemptive plans; His gave it all for a family, How can there be any more purity to this covenant. Today

both my parents preceded me to their heavenly home. Such assurance has brought freedom and trust to continue to lean into my eternal Father God. Later on, there were significant godly fathers and mothers divinely planted all throughout my life's journey. And I continue to be My Father's Daughter!

Jesus said: My Father has been working, until now, and I have been working! (John 5:17).

Next inspirational book coming soon:

<u>In The Moment of His Moment coming</u>

Reflections:

God is calling nations as well as individuals and He hasn't stopped calling! Are you being still enough and available to hear His voice?

CHAPTER 3

AMAZING BODY
KEEPS SCORES.

———————◆———————

When I become interested in connecting emotional trauma with disease development, the best resources I can recommend is below. I suffered from a concussion, and I had literally attended seminars on this topic, but few are like the three sources I will reference and experienced. In one form or the other, the physical manifestation of a disease process has its origin in thoughts, memories, and historical events.

Some are post-traumatic stress disorder (PTSD) which is a complex condition that requires specialized care and treatment. There are various resources available for people who suffer from PTSD, including books, online resources, and professional treatment. It is important to understand that PTSD is a complex condition, even with the best references, seeking professional treatment from a trained mental health professional is vital not just for the patient but also for the support of the family.

The following resources are the best references for PTSD:

Dr. Bessel Ven der Volk: Unhealed trauma, maladjusted personalities, and now mental illness.

Yes, the stress will ultimately kill you. The anger and bitterness will distort all your better judgement: loss of mental acuity. Then the shame and guilt are twins meant to shut you down.

How does the body keep scores? The body is not just organs and parts casually thrown together. God is not the one who stays in harmony with lies. He is the lover of the law of love, and not the lover of the law. (He is not into splitting hair legalism).

Once someone tried to shut me up and began accusing me that I postulated whenever I shared the goodness of God. I sensed within the accuser the effects of previous condemnations, or shame from other sources. In other words, much deeper hurts with accompanying lies, they had not been acknowledged or heard. Without forgiveness of self and others, truth be told, so many churches or organizational wounds remain unhealed. I was one of those, before I had developed a faith journey with God. Deep healing needs qualified professional counselors, and it may take years. It was really the <u>message stirring up hidden unresolved pain</u>, concealed, neatly packaged titles and achievements. The deep well has not allow the fresh life to spring up. Often it is not about the messenger but the response to the message and not always against the person, Dr Bessel explained the demeanor of the intolerance to those around. 7.70. I asked only once why to forgive 7 x 70 times. I received a deeper impression that was unforgettable as well as insightful: There are so many angles to look at within a person or situation as only God can see. Life offers multi-layered, even multi-dimensional unexamined depth to every background and uniqueness. My mind's eye immediately saw the spinning of a Rubik's cube. I sensed a reply from Father: "I created all, and I see all the transcendence of my creation and at every angle". How many angles do you see Mary? What can you create apart from me? I rest my case; so now, I ask this question, can you create dirt?

Traumatized boy/how he turned south:

Many years ago, I worked at an integrative medical center. Being in medical aesthetic, I helped men or women in post reconstructive surgeries with some transdermal procedures some of which are injectables, some people had been over medicated, and the skin have been neglected. The fact is that a well cleansed canvas is appropriate for men and women.

An interesting well-built man near 6-foot-tall, friendly and appearing very kindly, he wished to be shown some facial cleansing regiments, but it didn't stop there, he wanted more… I was unaware that one of our integrative doctors, a German trained East Coast physician, had an ambitious plan way beyond bio-identical hormone therapies but now he had bumped against my moral boundary very quickly. Sex change procedures were very foreign to a mid-western town where he was otherwise an excellent physician, patients loved his most caring demeanor. However, he had plans that I would be part of his transition team. During my initial two appointments Doug (not his real name), from the soft instrumental music playing in my office, he remarked that he was a worship leader and he felt peace. Doug continued recounting his childhood trauma; His father, a church associate leader, had daily witnessed physically abused his mother and essentially, refuse to grow up in a man's body suit like his dad. Conveniently the center has a specialist who offered Doug a chance to "self-actualize". He also erroneously assigned me to secure family supports on subsequent appointments on my schedule. Even more presumptuously, he offered me to be the makeup instructor for the small band of men on his same journey. I kept my professional composure all the while I knew what I have to do. I interrupted him, and firmly informed him the boundaries I had at my practice. Just as he stood up to leave, so I thought, he abruptly knelt on the floor with overwhelming tears of contrition, even deep repentance I had not heard before. I gently side stepped away from his body motioned that his time is up, but I assured Doug that God is pleased with repentance.

Mr. Doug's last visit was full of drama with a gift of flowers and a more significant financial offer suggesting that I just have to show mercies to a group of boys who never really discovered their femininity. He's in the race car male dominated business, and well able to afford the four years of psychological counseling before the actual anatomical procedure begins. The transitioning of hormonal and physical alterations was a cruel process. My "No" to a lot of other things or people are affirming my "Yes" to God.

Just before Doug's next appointment, as I entered my office, I found an envelope with a poem and a request to meet off sight to discuss my future career. Now, I thank God for unusual grace, I greeted Mr. Doug; "Have a chair sir, I then looked intently at him as though my eyes talked first: Mr. Doug, you are handsome, healthy and if I were a younger woman, I would have wish to date a good man like you. However, I will not...., I will not...., I am not for sale. I am not accepting any flowers, the receptionists are told to send them away and if you continue to drop gifts at the front desk, the girls have strict orders from me not to accept but to the garbage bin. This is our last appointment, and it is on me, therefore, there is no charge. According to your chart, I consulted with your Dr. B. sir, you have a chance to stop further treatment now. It's reversable as of today! Keep your beautiful poems for your future wife. I see you with beautiful children and leading a most satisfying family life. Dr. B had known me to have experience teaching at facial plastic surgeon's convention, but I am not part of his team! Our patient client relationship just ended this minute. Good day! What followed was a non-negotiable conversation with Doug's doctor, normally he shown much courteous professionalism towards me, had now become a chameleon. I quietly and politely left his office suite very relieved. Within 48 hours I individually visited with the 3 other doctors' and therapists my decision to close my practice. Also urgently ask everyone all be ready to relocate their office sooner than later. (Without sharing my reason of my abrupt departure), I was amazed that within three months, everyone left the team except Dr. B who had no choice but to buy the whole building. Which house over 15 clinical offices with conference room and staff lounges. Less than three years later, a close associate shared a newspaper obituary informing me that the owner doctor had an unfortunate death. It then confirmed to me my God-fearing sense to warn all to relocate was not just a feeling, and the integrative clinic sat idle with no buyer!

It's about the heart response that directs changes including caring for our body. This is very spiritual, coming from the inside out, there really is an orderly manner to maintain wellness in all levels of Spirit, Soul, and Body connections. There are plenty of wonderful teachings available. It's like the law of gravity, violations will have consequences. Ever wonder how a worship leader repented and keep on the spiral down path? Is apostasy happening due to hardened hearts?

Meditate on: Roman 1:30-32 Covenant is important to God and us. Self-deception is everywhere, wrongly relatedness can be deadly, pick your friends and associates carefully, casual soulish-ties will bring casualties. Its the swimmer that sinks. I Corinthian 10:23 All things are lawful, but not all things are edifying for me.

We are birthed from heaven and can miss the mark, who doesn't? We are not sinners. When it's interchangeably used in the Bible, <u>Sin</u> is a noun and of an entity, an influencer of evil against humanity. Its missions are acts of violations against God, against His people (self and others) as all diseases are originally curse incurred. Diseases are not a blessing, while we live on this earth, absence of diseases is blessing. We are to choose life or death, blessings, or curses (Deuteronomy 30:19-20). Don't let offense or even a lifetime of offense turn you from anger to bitter self-hatred.

In addition, Dr Christian Waugh, Ph.D. at Wake Forest University, N.C. study of stress resilience in the field of Affective Neuroscience:

Exaggerated Self-Appraisal: narcissism, the pathology of perfectionism and self-righteous individuals, worry about worrying. Some keys: By cultivating playfulness and attaining contentment.

Psalms 103:3 says "He forgives ALL my iniquities (generational' personalities, gender tendencies can be wired in; He healed ALL my diseases. In this one verse, we have <u>both forgiveness of sins</u> and the <u>true healing of disease</u> all, ALL together are available if you receive.

Dr. Henry Wright whom I met at <u>www.BeinHealth.com</u>

Meditating on Psalms 103:3 - He forgives and heals ALL. Now it's our turn to appropriate the exchange the divine exchange to receive inheritance as joint heirs.

Faith currency rewarded: I remembered that I had to jump out of my religious jailhouse. Refer to Chapter 4 Drips of Resentment, it was a fight of faith. Forgiveness in conjunction with disease prevention. Including nutritional supports that are keys to keep our healing testimonies on going. In life, nothing is guaranteed to be smooth sailing, I am not promised perfect health in this body, while living among the cesspool of deception but we can take the treasure from the vile.

I attended one of the many professional seminars in recent years, this information was from the Summer of 2014 (<u>www.ibpceu.com</u>) *by Dr. Joseph Shannon, Ph.D., Ohio State University, psychologist, clinician, research and lecturer in the areas of personality disorders, chemical dependency, character pathology, anxiety and depression.*

Understanding Anger: I was blown away that science has been catching up with God. Much of God's foundational principles and consequences are being displayed in Dr. Joseph Shannon's conference. He took time to discuss in real practical concepts, advances in applicable management skills for health care professionals. He brought reality and compassions to the panel discussion of understanding anger:

- About Maltreatment, abuse and trauma are re-lived as hurt, anger, sadness, and shame by way of wounding at any given time in life.

- How threat, empathy and the self-healing gift of forgiveness are organized in the brain.

- Anger and the Body: Physical conditions that lower the threshold for anger, e.g., chronic pain.

- Health Risks to patients with Chronic Anger and to their Caregivers, who work with Angry Clients: Hypertension, type 2 diabetes, coronary artery disease; muscle tension and upper and lower back pain; TMJ; immune suppression, disturbed sleep, and appetite; reduced longevity among many indications, e.g., reduction of DNA's telomere length.

- Thoughts that sustain Anger: What purpose does anger serve? Self-destructive thoughts maintaining anger.

Understanding Anger-and related Disorders

- Uninhibited Anger: diagnosing oppositional-defiant and conduct disorders.

- Disinhibited Anger: episodic and intermittent explosive subtypes.

- Chronic Low-Grade Anger: risks of "stuffing" negative emotions, the Type-C personality and cancer.

- From Mad to Sad-Anger Turned Inward: major depression, low grade dysthymic disorder; assessing risk of self-harm.

- Bipolar Disorders: three major forms; their neurological characteristics and treatments; mood swings and anger.

- Dissociated Anger: PTSD, depersonalization, triggers, and flashbacks.

- Impaired Empathy: the antisocial personality.

- Coping with Loss: the shift from sadness to anger, to dismissals of hope.

Since late teen, my work trained me in hospitality, then dental and plastic surgery as well as my own clinical and wellness practice, a total sum of 30 years (minus homemaking), my working observations bear witness to the above information. Below are summaries of my notes from Dr. Shannon's Seminar, the major theme was to cultivate a lifestyle of Forgiveness. He presented the connection between Forgiveness with disorders and disease, I hope the following resonates with you as it did with me:

1. Health benefits of Forgiveness enhance physical and mental health towards a quality of life.

2. Identify how we unwittingly reward behaviors that engender and sustain such anger, and therefore block forgiveness, involving self-discovery.

3. Creating boundaries: identifying who we should interact under what circumstances.

4. Preludes to Forgiveness: Reconciliation is not required.

5. Barriers to Forgiveness: Recognizing that it is the memory of the offense and not the original wound that blocks our ability to forgive.

6. Creating Words That Facilitate Meaningful Change.

7. Confiding: Ability to express feeling and thoughts to trusted confidants.

8. Expressive Writing: Choose health benefits of self-expression.

There is so much more involved in cognitive Behavioral Therapy, habitual Anger-evoking Thoughts and reframing these thoughts. Learn to identify traits in others that are unlikely to change and keep moving on. Continue cultivating that happy people harness to elevate mood, stress, and resilience, learning with humility by asking for help. Keep in touch with your purpose, every day stay true to your core values, including your surroundings, trusting faith to facilitate forgiveness. Finally, For I, nourish that little girl's child likeness to co-create with the Father.

Why, do you mean I can die from this?

(Example of my brief encounter with a nurse)

Let's call this lady nurse Cici (not her real name), she started working at her new job at a hospital I was acquainted with. We crossed path in the hallway, I extended my greeting, and I asked if she was new. She related about her relocation to a new city and new job. Also, Cici was very eager to share her real reason for her relocation. It was due to a finalized divorce proceeding within a couple of months ago and she sounded determined to resettle with a new environment.

The conversation was a one-sided brief introduction of her swift relocation, but Cici added that made good from the settlement, while I sensed her victory, I had a slight uneasiness. I reassured her she's blessed to have a good place to work and congratulated her. Back then, the hospital was famous as the best employer and won state and even national recognitions. That was a short sixty second encounter, we each must return to work.

This is not an exaggerated estimation of time: In about 6-8 weeks time, I heard the report that nurse Cici who just got started had taken an irreversible turn from cancer and died very unexpectedly! My thoughts were, why? And how so suddenly! Did she win the battle and lose the war???

The take home message here is, don't allow the enemy of your soul to take you out. Its purpose is to come steal, kill and destroy you.

Let me just take these 3 words and expand a little:

<u>Steal</u>: your personal property, credit card, your car, etc. Inconveniences of all kinds, but nonetheless, most can be replaced. But it will cost you time, with family and from work, distractions.

<u>Kill</u>: from stressors to life threatening, costing you distresses, costing you expenses with no returns. The stress of loss of loved ones, worries and anxieties, a sudden loss of career, etc.

<u>Destroy</u>: Any message or actions of alienation of any kind! Jealousy, accusations of your identity (especially from gossips), deeply brewing from the above two: steal, kill. Any drug or addictions of choice. Prolong hopelessness and lack of skills, leaving you defendless, gossip intending to destroy any covenant relationship communities. Devastating mistrust issues. And deeply imbedded unforgiveness, it's an investor who made small and large deposits which will ultimately take you down, irrational thinking and isolations, evilness demand withdraws by your volunteering.

Decide ahead of time why you say YES, and to whom you are saying yes to. Detour quickly (if you have given your heart to the wrong place, people pleasing, and comparisons self-sabotaging).

Cognitive Dissonance: Psychological conflict resulting from incongruous beliefs and attitudes held simultaneously. A term I learned in college, settle once and for all who you are, and whose you belong to, what you do, and what are your why? Who taught you to negotiate away your most precious self? You are worth dying for, and it's paid in full before you discover you have a thumb and enjoy sucking on it. Furthermore, those who attempt to encroach on my identity must have my permission. Don't lease your mental and emotional space to just anyone. No trespassing on my boundaries.

Self-awareness: Discern if self-deception has been your default pathway. We all know people and even leaders on many levels calling good evil. Subtly brings a title deed to occupy room by room to own your true self, mostly to take advantage of the injustice or broken spaces you have suffered, to creating your own sinkhole. No, God didn't do it, you unknowingly allow the thief into the rooms of your house. The best way to be intentional about knowing yourself, honesty with God and self is a high functioning self-developed skill especially in challenging times, make sure you have quality friends who can speak truth even if it's painful to hear, deception is a blinder. Not everyone is allow, you must seek it and not just anyone, God can direct you to the right one, learn to ask good questions, make room to ask the Holy Spirit to counsel and comfort.

I ask myself questions, Merry Mary, how's your garden growing? This growing work takes meditative time and solitude for His small still voice, it's the reason for being still, to know and also be known to the One who always and eternally loves me.

Supernatural healings are available with revelations from heaven to earth, every day we are surrounded by the goodness of God. Especially when I posture my heart's identity as His daughter, that posture is one of receiving grace to cultivate, mature between seasons, changes, adapt and be reformed, not conform to everyone's agendas.

I find Dr. Mike Hutching's perspectives on freedom are most relevant along with this image given to me from the Japanese Kintsugi vase by a life coach. Kintsugi, also known as Kintsukuori, is the Japanese art of repairing broken pottery by mending and putting back together the areas of breakage with lacquer dusted or mixed with 22 karat powdered gold, silver or platinum. The flaw reveals its history of brokenness.

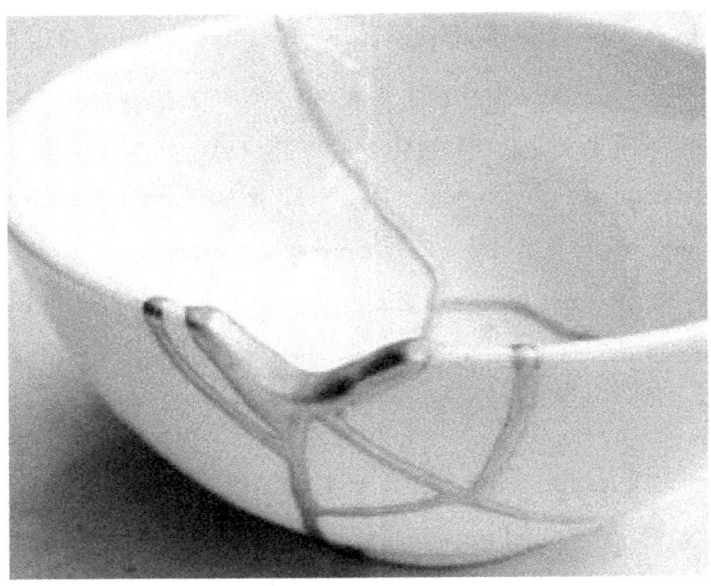

Once the broken pieces of a vase, a dish, the Master Artist will only use gold to infuse the broken pieces together, the Master has a plan to display His now most precious artwork, no longer to be casually used but He displays with gold and the value is now far higher with His signature on the artwork, you are a priceless piece of His work.

"God is here to heal you and take the shattered pieces of your broken heart and put them back together again. He is here to restore you and give you a life of freedom and purpose so that you can walk out in peace all the days of your life. He is eager to cast off the false identity you have been struggling under and reveal your true God-given identity to you because God has plans for you," a quote from the book Captivity of Trauma by Mike Hutchings.

"For I know the plans I have for you," declares the Lord,
"plans to prosper you and not to harm you, plans to
give you hope and a future" (Jeremiah 29:11)

We ask because there are areas of ourselves, we have not known before, there is a divine exchange, if we let Him in…In-to-me see, sounds like intimacy, because I am my Father's Daughter.

Thoughts to ponder:

Are you a gatherer of disappointments, especially from others' injustices because you have an empathetic and a heightened sensitivity of the gift of mercy?

How do you distinguish a false responsibility from the real one? How do you know if you are honest with yourself?

CHAPTER 4

DRIPS OF RESENTMENTS

———————◆———————

Fatal Drips of Resentment: No matter how smart, how educated, how fast you can figure it out, the entrapment only gets deeper. How much you perform cannot compare to the pearl of the great price of knowing the One who has paid it forward for all races and for all eternity!

Why do I bring this up? Because I failed the forgiveness test at team USA in a major manner! Ignorantly, as I learned my lesson, I also gained victory over death.

Jesus gave me victory over my history, Healing of the physical, is more about receiving and accessing faith, the heavenly currency of embracing trust, mindful of everything bursting of hope, the kingdom pathfinder is faith from an intimate rested trust on Ephesian, all from a rested posture of Ephesian 2:26, I sat down between my Father and my Brother, JESUS, the first earth borne of the Tri-unity, he became like me...Now my prayer advocate who was my defender when evil had an open entrance to contend for my life. The sinful action or attitude of unforgiveness opened a path for Sin to come and collect his dues, to steal, kill and destroy. I was raised in the convent full of nuns during most of my primary school years and mostly throughout high school, I thought what a waste, our face ought to be the canvas of the image we bear. Therefore, I took interest to enjoy cosmetics. I had a fun season studying about skincare. There is so much about a well cleansed face, how it reflects spectrum of lights is very fascinating. I enjoyed a season of being in the skincare and cosmetics business, so much so the company paid for my formal apprenticeship with a very famous Hollywood movie FX makeup artist, she suggested me to be a part of a wedding extravaganza. Upon discovering that I had to leave my family to pursue some "black book" makeup artistry, I had no appetite for that world, the instructor warned me that it will erode your character if you are not careful. But I prayed not to be a part of it, as it turned out the whole thing got canceled.

Being surrounded by fashions, travels and meeting all kinds of truly beautiful women. But there was no shortage of crazies even among the beautiful, sophisticated women. Jealousy, discrimination, drugs, bizarre behaviors, the worst are the self-appointed spiritual police. all mixed into almost 4 years of fun and dramas. One can grow old and not grow up! I walked the walk and now I can talk the talk!

Offense to Trauma: It is a conglomerate of uninvited guests sharing my space, helping itself to my health, I felt the slow drips running down both sides of my neck. I remembered speaking up that in a business world of beauty. How can the ugliest behaviors show up.

I could feel something was wrong around my neck for a while, not knowing I made room for the lymph to grow to the size of a small tangerine, swell up just below my chin. It was a pre-lymphoma mass collected and swelling inwardly and outwardly, no wonder I was given 3-4 days, at that time, surgery would result in me sounding like Dath-Vader if it could save my life, at the rate of growth, I would die of suffocation. (We now understand stress and anxiety, a wide range of serious illnesses, current understanding of gut brain dis-eases, breakdown on the cellular level, incessant pain like their nerves is on fire, then cancer, etc.)

I was immediately admitted through the E.R. on July 18-21, 1999. The team of doctors gently advised my physician husband and I to gather immediate next of kins, etc., but being that mine were all overseas. The cancer specialist and the E.N.T. specialist, Dr. Snow, (during the writing of this book, we talked with him, who since retired.) at that time, he nudged my husband sympathetically and advised him to prepare for the worst!

Somehow, I didn't experience any fear. But I decided to gather with God first, and I calmly told my husband not to frighten the children, they are too young to know, and I believed even this shall pass!!! I was considered as going off the deep end. I was ignorant and I sent all the flowers away from the hospital staff, none of my friends, neighbors nor my pastor were contacted. What I wanted was no accursed words declared over me, such as "Oh, how terrible, your kids are so young, and your parents and family are so far away...." Chatter noise can interfere with my healing. In truth, when I see a wound, I asked for discernment to reveal the source of the wound, even in 1999, I was learning many lessons. Notes from a teaching I heard that I journaled from Dr. Adrian Rogers, Pastor of Belville Baptist Church, Tennessee. And I had the following conversation with God:

"Lord, I am not ready to join you yet, I am not ready to leave my two children, they need me, and I love them. For 3 days and 2 nights I asked for my desired outcome to be healed, I was given no other options. I took a bold step not to accept the symptoms presented by the brilliant and caring doctors. Funny that I have been collecting healing scriptures and recorded on an old fashion tape recorder.

My Father heard my cry and I have been keeping my healing testimony alive since then. This is the story of how I was given a very special grace to navigate from admission to discharge. There is a key distinction while I recognized I am placed in a death struggle. Or is it a sanitized fight? A fight of faith fights differently for only one walks away alive." Christ Jesus is an unbridled force. Grace is always working; He is already there! Jesus Christ is not a Christian, but my brother, and we share the same blood. He shows up when there's the doer of the Word, let Him out. Grace is the power that removes dead things where death tenaciously hang on.

Praying in tongues by the power of the Holy Spirit for three days, and given the interpretation of what He wants for me, I slept little. I just had IV fluid to sustain me, but I had so much energy and hope filled expectancy that I didn't feel sick, hungry nor thirsty. I looked good even in the ugly hospital gown. One nurse came and encouraged me, with the script for pain meds. I flushed them down the toilet after she left the room. Then another very sweet nurse came trying to comfort me, her kindness led me to inquire of her faith, in short, she believed me, and she received the baptism of the Holy Spirit because she asked the right question about my prayer language!

After the first 24 hours, I pushed my IV cart and marched forth toward the nursing station (seeing my ENT Doc, there among several nurses). I greeted them cheerfully, and they turned towards me:

"Dr. Snow, I am not ready to leave, I will see my children grow up, I will live to see grandchildren. I 've got people to see and places to go, I just want you all to know, I will not accept this death sentence…." He turned around, ever so gentlemanly gave me this reply: "THAT 'a Girl, Mrs. Axness." Dr. Snow equated my voice with the same decibel. And another doctor came in trying to comfort me. I sensed a force pushed out of me to redefine the atmosphere. When the doctor didn't patronize nor mock my declarations. I considered I have the Amen and it's accomplished!

With that out of the way, I joyfully went back to my room, pushing my IV, marching around, continued to be energized by praying in tongues. I sensed joy and peace, so much so, I unbolted my room again, and marched down the hallway, ask room to room, anyone who wants prayer? I probably prayed with one! I wasn't crazy. Deep within a renewed roaring to finish in triumph. Then I laid down to rest a bit. That afternoon, the pathology report came back that there is nothing, everything shrunk and dissipated. Yes, there were antibiotic in the IV., Almighty God healed me, the doctors cooperated with me. No meds, no surgery, no flowers, no sympathy, no scare for my kids. But the angels were singing my song.

The fourth day I was discharged when all the swelling went down (there was a small 1" size incision" where a biopsy was done.) They couldn't find anything wrong. So, I was discharged with a small gauze covering the biopsy stitches. I was told to return in 2 weeks to the Dr. Snow's office for a recheck and to remove the stitches.

So, my sweet daughter came home from college to assist my discharge, and my husband kept on working the whole time. She is my awesome child, even now, she's always by me. I could not leave my kids; I keep seeing in my faith's lens that I will see them through. I swallow tears backwards when my girl showed up to bring me home. Truthfully, I insisted she stop off at our Sunday school teacher's house whose wife, Sylvia, struggled with cancer for several years. While my daughter waited outside, I took liberty to practically invited myself into their home and prayed for her. My hands and feet were so hot, she went limp, resting in the Spirit and I said goodbye. (It took about 7 minutes.) But I could tell her husband was in disbelief because he was exhausted from being a caregiver.

Two weeks passed, I showered only from my chest down, I returned to my doctor's office, as he removed the gauze, my doctor admonished me that, I should not be pulling out the stitches. I replied that I did no such thing. He said there were no stitches to remove, I grinned from ear to ear. The doctor was not believing me, but I could tell, he really was scratching his head. And I was so blessed that there were hardly any incision scars.

I had the green light to part from the team USA, but I continued to have a good relationship with a few ladies. It was 4 years of accelerated opportunities and much oppressiveness. In the end, the company bought out my small portion of the business. They reassured me that I would have a good standing with them and to return anytime.

A root of offense and unforgiveness caused me such physiological imbalance that it almost took my life. This is my first-hand supernatural healing miracle I experienced in July of 1999. Only my husband and the pathology report can vouch for me. We did not have cell phones and cameras, or I would have kept pictures and journals of my entire experience.

Personally, I had a distaste for emotional drama. I went to the extreme of being a very tight-lipped person. It was my 70th birthday before I shared my childhood openly, mainly because I was very focused on being a wife, and a mother. And I could tell, people are more self-focused, it was an unusual challenge to be married to an overly devoted physician, in a mixed raced marriage. After my precious mother-in-love passed, I had a pack of 5 merciless jealous women, (I went out of my way to keep connection over 30 years to no avail, they relentlessly trying to dismantle my marriage!) moving around the years made it difficult to explore quality friendships. Also, there can be unwanted sympathy, which is deploring, empathy would be caring, but I needed my time with the One Who holds the key to life. I kept journals like a reporter or a scribe!

Several years passed, as I was enjoying good health when I asked my Father God:

1. What part did I play resulting in this sudden growth and horrible diagnosis?
2. How can I avoid the same devastating onslaught?
3. Finally, what is needed to keep my healing miracle?

Whenever I ask good questions, His simple replies are fittingly to my easy understanding:

His answer #1: Mary, you did not create the stress, but in your responses to the stressors (people), you got entangled in the hurt and held unforgiveness of others and yourself, truth be told, you've been devalued, and thought not to bother others, that attitude is pride. Hard to hear but deep down, it's true.

His answer #2: Some onslaughts are unavoidable, not everyone knows how to appreciate or even reciprocate your loyalty. Don't keep swimming with them. Ok, Dad, in other words, prioritize and allocate your YES.

His answer #3: You keep your testimony alive and keep a servant leader's heart. (10 leapers got healed, and only one foreigner returned to give thanks!)

Subsequent conversations with my God about my healing led me to produce a teaching video on "Delicious Enzymes" a way to feed the body according to its design. I also completed my degree in Naturopath N.D., to keep leading more awareness to optimized wellness. I am thankful every day while continuing to learn more about ways to help disease prevention. This video is a way to prepare fresh food keeping the highest degree of enzymes' potentials. Testimony means please do it again Lord, for me and others. Remembering my mother's loving admonition to her children was: If my children even think of putting anything that brings harm than good to their minds and bodies, that would be a mockery and acts of treasonous dishonor of her motherhood and her sacrificial loving legacy to the family. These words still ring true with me today.

Today, there are few teachings of forgiveness with disease prevention. Therefore, whenever possible, support your healing testimonies by combining with practical applications with daily quality foods to upgrade your quality of life. Finally, science is catching up with God's principles:

> If we get bitter toward those who offend us, we will damage our health and our enemies will control our thoughts and emotions. If we do good to them, we free God to handle them where they are at and bless us. *"Vengeance is mine; I will repay says the Lord . . . overcome evil with good"* (Roman 12:19-20 NKJV).

CHAPTER 5

PREPARATION FOR REUNION

———————◆———————

W hat is Impossible with men is possible with God: Remember the earthly dad whom I was so ashamed of? How I had to draw serious boundaries while being very respectful to both parents? When I had become a committed believer with the most supernatural encounter with God's presence in my bedroom, I began to read the Word daily in BSF (Bible Study Fellowship). I meditated throughout my day and never stop praying good towards my dad without denying what took place.

Since I had deep awareness of my relational deficiencies with my dad, I was intentionally committed to grow and make up for the loss of time. The Holy Spirit led me to a two-year intense study; "*The Exchanged Life*" based on the book of Galatians 2:19-21. This was every week, 4 hours of coaching, counseling and journaling. The Spirit of God discipled me as soon as I was born again, and not knowing, I processed inner-healing and grew in my reality as a brand-new creation. Humbly I grew in statue and favor with God and men. After 2 years of studying practical means to apply the Bible, a short get away marked a life journey of personal transformation which I teach within my private group! My surrendering of having to explain away every condition was heavier than the disease itself. I listened and RECEIVE, be a receiver!

Forgive all suspicion, fear and doubts and unbelieve, for your own health and maximize your life. Anticipation of good also means prepared for bad; Trusting His goodness and mercy will follow you everywhere. Heaven ready but still work hard, clean house, and living every day to its fullest!

As a colonist born and raised in Hong Kong, I persevered through all the proper process that took about 12 years to consider the decision of becoming a US Citizen when an event happened at the San Francisco Airport. After returning from a family visit to Hong Kong when my daughter was 4 years old, upon arrival at the US immigrations, after long flights and exhaustion, my child and I were separated because she was a natural born citizen, and I was a "Green Card" non-citizen status. We had to be in two separate lines differentiated by either "US Citizen" (my daughter) or "Alien" (myself), momentarily waiting to pass through to customs (about 20 feet apart). I instructed my daughter that "momma sees you and stand still" as we kept maintaining eye contact. I chatted with a uniformed officer, being very concerned and insisting that we stay together. Throughout the trip having been inseparable, I could tell she was beginning to tear up. The officer led her to join me at the non-citizen's line. I took a sigh with relief, thinking all is well and I was ready to retrieve our luggage for the next connecting flight. Then I got this tug on my side with my daughter motioning me to bend down so I can hear her whisper her concern; "Momma, what is an "alien"? My girl had always excelled in language. At age 2 while in diapers, she read the newspaper and learned that Macy's department store had a big sale going on. She would grab my purse and wanted me to take her to the sale. Its amazing she never pick up the newspaper ads on grocery specials!!!

Later, on a continuing flight I discovered my daughter spelled the word alien to me. I reassured her that momma was not an alien even for a few minutes. However, that incident propelled me to petition for my US Citizenship, and never again be separated from my children.

Once that was settled, I suddenly realized I can begin to sponsor my mother for a green card visitation so she could visit freely come and go. However, my dad decided to come along. The manner of his behavior had never improved with regards to my own family but after visiting with my family, I sensed a calmness and offered him a round trip ticket with an open return date. Yes, I prayed for God's perfect will because I sensed an assurance that God had my best interests. I really surrendered.

In the shadow of my hurt, forgiveness feels like a decision to reward my enemy.
But in the shadow of the cross, forgiveness is merely a gift from one undeserving soul to another.

—

Suddenly, two weeks before their arrival, I was to meet them on the west coast while we were residing in the Midwest. I got a phone call via my siblings that our dad had decided <u>not</u> to come with my mother. I had mixed emotions, but I believed God had intervened in a major way. My mother's arrival was a special time for all of us. She enjoyed time with the grandkids and most evenings, we enjoyed her authentic Asian home cooking. This provided my kids a special and wonderful bond with their grandmother.

Sadly, my father never really changed, but I accepted that he was in God's special care. While mother was in the US with us, it gave an opportunity for my 3 siblings to move my dad away to distance them from each other because the domestic abuse had continued. My siblings paid all his living expenses and furnished him with his own housing. My siblings pulled together resources for dad to have a separate address. It was quite an undertaking for them but after mom stayed with me in the US for more than a year, she felt safe to return to be near her 3 grown children. We were all relieved that mom could live in peace.

After mom's arrival in the US, within one month, we had the most special mother-daughter time. One afternoon, my mom asked how I had become happy and productive. She observed that I had become very different, and she was so curious about what had happened to her daughter! I proceeded to explained how I had forgiven my dad, but I couldn't stay in Hong Kong to be a part of their marital dysfunction. She also came to understand I desired to grow and maximize God's wishes in my life. Within an hour of conversation, mom said <u>she wanted what I have</u>!!! You had heard that before however this was a privilege to lead my own mom to invite Christ Jesus into her heart at the age of 59. Mother earnestly fell in love with The Lord and her Savior reading her Bible as though it was the greatest treasure daily. She honestly was having a difficult time forgiving my dad; therefore, I became sort of her spiritual mother for a whole year, along with some local church friends. She was discipled during this time and an excellent learner of the principle of the exchanged life. She forgave her husband from her heart and released him to God! She shed many tears for the next few weeks as I proceeded to share with her the difference between forgiveness and reconciliation. I watched my own mother transformed while she was in the Word daily. I shared what I was learning and encouraged her to show me more, as well as leading her to pray. One year later, I could tell she was missing my siblings and was ready to return home. She told me that she wanted to share the good news in her community in Hong Kong.

Indeed, she became quite an evangelist in her district. Watching her become free and well cared for by her children, she not only forgave but she did not compromise her own standards. Later, my grandma asked for forgiveness from my mom. My mother then led my grandma, (my dad's mother) to Jesus a few months before she peacefully passed. This was the same grandma who took me to the most miserable temple outings. I will get to see the best version of her some day!

Regarding my dad, I am fully persuaded that my dad is already waiting for us! How could I be so sure? <u>Forgiveness makes way for God to do what He does best</u>. Several years later, I received a phone call from my youngest brother, informing me that my dad had a fall while visiting my uncles inside China. Mom's seven other siblings hired a couple to care for him. The phone call notified me that he was to have a hip replacement. I took the opportunity to tell my brothers to forgive dad and for us to pray together for his healing. In addition, my brother proceeded to tell me that dad wanted reconciliation with mom. Once discharged after surgery, he wished to invite all her families for a dinner, wondering if our mom would join in. My reply was that mom would be the only one to make such a decision. I did remind them, however, that I hadn't seen my dad for over 25 years. Trusting for God to work everything out for good, I felt peace and a sense of anticipation of good things to come. Two days later, my brother called again to tell me that the surgery had gone well, dad would be discharged in a few days. We were most grateful for his quick recovery. Another phone call from my brother shared that he would pick dad up when there's a known discharge date and we prayed on the phone again!

It was clear that my baby brother didn't know what to expect from our distanced dad. It would take several hours of travel for them to meet up, before my dad was ready to be discharged. While waiting for the doctors to sign off, my dad decided to lay down for a short nap while waiting for his younger son to assist the discharge. He was all dressed up and instructed the nurse to wake him up when his son arrived. However, my dad slept his way to his heavenly home!

I received the call from my brother that dad passed most peacefully while napping. My brother took special care to related to me he believed our prayer, and how he witnessed our dad's face glowing with almost baby skin and rosy cheeks. He didn't even believe that he had passed. It was not a most welcomed call, but both my brother and I were assured that God heard our prayers; we prayed that his natural health be invigorated.

When my baby brother reported what he saw, there were no words to describe my emotions other than grace reaching deep down all these years of praying to release toxic emotions. I recall that afternoon, I had shared with someone that my dad had passed and briefly recapturing my prayers. That person got saved right there! It was a double blessing for me that God is trust worthy and He heard!

An unusual recalling that my brother and I didn't go through the normal grieving process. We had a very settled peace that our dad is with the One who knows how to love him better than any of us. Another confirmation was when I met up with my uncles in China years later, they said it was a good thing that our dad had initiated reconciliation with the whole family. They confided that the couple whom they hired to care for my dad because of his fall, were a known dedicated Christian couple whom my dad was most fond of, and my dad became very pleasant to everyone around! I stand on this Word in Acts 16:31; Believe on the Lord Jesus Christ, and you will be saved, you and your whole household.

Furthermore, I was given a watercolor painting of my dad, recognizing his handwriting and his style. The family thought I should have it as he had written in Chinese: For God so loved the world, he gave His only begotten Son, that whoever believes in Him should not perish but have everlasting life. Any wonder why I am so passionate about evangelism and discipleship?!

After serving on multiple inner healing streams and ministries, gratefully I continue to learn and lead others (Ephesian 1:7) to repent and release offenses. True forgiveness is from the heart to release the <u>offender</u> to

Almighty God's dealings. Set aside time or get with a trusted prayer minister experienced in inner healing. If none is available, be still and reverently invite the Spirit of God, the Counselor, the Teacher and The Comforter to guide you, one item at a time to release the effects, the message of mis-profiling to distort your God given identity. Discern who you are <u>soul-tied</u> to. Blaming or unforgiveness eventually can turn you to become the very person you despised - quit making anything or anyone your god!

Pray this: Father God, Because of your merciful forgiveness, and thank you for forgiving me of all my sins (I Corinthians 11:28a) including 3rd/4th generations past. I also want to release my offenders to you by forgiving them. Listen and wait on the good Father for the impressions/voice of assurance to continue....

A sample Prayer to release forgiveness to my underserving parent:

1. I forgive you, ___for misrepresenting God to me.
2. I forgive you, ___for rejecting my conception and birth as an inconvenience.
3. I forgive you, ___for pressuring me to your agenda against my calling.
4. I forgive you, ___for giving me a skewed view of marriage.
5. I forgive you, ___for not protecting me when I need you.
6. I forgive you, ___for your selfishness by not prioritizing your time with me.
7. I forgive you, ___for opening the door of fear, and abandonment.

8. I forgive you, ___for not being there when I needed you as my cheerleader.

9. I forgive you, ___for being slothfulness, lacking the example I needed.

10. I forgive you, ___for opening the door for worthlessness.

11. I forgive you, ___for not being a good listener when I needed you to hear me.

12. I forgive you, ___for deceitfulness, your words and deeds are incongruent.

13. I forgive you, ___ for not teaching me how to trust in relationships.

Feel free to add to your own list if or when needed.

Pray for your offender: I release ___to hear God's voice and ___ do His will.

Now, a sample <u>prayer for yourself</u>: Father God, I release ___for their ignorance, I do not keep any part of them what does not belong to me! I give you Jesus Lord God every darkness You have paid for on my behalf on the cross. Now, there is no barrier between us Lord God, therefore I boldly and confidently ask that you bring to death and dismiss any charges from any "old ways" of responding and reacting to stress, shock, trauma, fear or terror. Dismantle the ungodly structures of defenses and mistrusts. I ask you now for new neurological connections to my joy center. Rebuild within me (your name ___), Now godly structures based on Your Word: Reframe and recalibrate trust and understanding of my spiritual authority as a son/daughter of the Most High God. Please fill every cell and memory with your peace and healing grace of Your pure design. Displace all darkness with Your light. Keep me, _____ in your perfect peace, also in the night seasons when I rest, send heavenly angelic protection to guard me, _____ as I sleep and quiet me, _____ with your Love. Christ Jesus, I take back my God given blueprint and all that Father has purposed for me. Thank you for Your redemptive plans and revelation knowledge of my future, my ordained purpose. (Meditation: Psalm 139).

Congratulations, Journal your victory over your history.

_____

Now, you are a brave heart and well able to carry out the assignments and shore up for your generations. You may desire to mark this day with heavenly bread in remembrance for His abundant life. You do not need permission to receive Holy Communion to partake of the Bread and wine/juice is your remembrance of Christ Jesus.

Scriptural meditations:

I Thessalonians 5:23 Sanctified wholly, whole being: spirit, soul, body be preserved.

Ephesians 1:17-21 Revelation and knowledge

Galatians: 2:19-21 Divine Exchange Life.

Ephesian: 2:6 Seated and secured and rested.

Luke 22:18-19 Do this in remembrance the Body and Blood of Christ Jesus.

II Corinthians 11:25-26 In remembrance as <u>often</u> as you desire.

Psalms 139:1-6; v.13-18 (you are his chosen love before time, now and for eternity). None of the prayers above are a sudden magic wand, for some of you, the breakthrough can be very real, for some it may take weeks. Your part is to pursue with your whole heart to draw near, your receiving attitude will attract heaven and God's attention. The matter is settled, you are His chosen one! Please connect to a church community, ask your Father to show you who can mentor you and be respectful that even the most respected authorities, they are still growing, do not judge a tree by its season.

Say out loud: I speak peace, love and abundant grace and blessings over you, (your name _____). And continue to speak good things over yourself.

Earnest love and richest blessings!

Video testimony from Dr. Mike Hutchings (Overcoming the Hindrance to Your Wholeness):

https://youtu.be/uzoaqgYSXGg